PANZER
GRENADIERS

JAMES LUCAS AND MATTHEW COOPER

PANZER GRENADIERS

MACDONALD ILLUSTRATED WAR STUDY

BOOK CLUB ASSOCIATES

This edition published by
Book Club Associates
by arrangement with
Macdonald and Jane's

Design: Judy Tuke
Maps: Cyril McCann MBE

Phototypeset by Trident Graphics Ltd, Reigate, Surrey

Printed in Great Britain by
REDWOOD BURN LIMITED
Trowbridge & Esher

Contents

To *General der Infanterie* Hubert Wingelbauer, the Defence Attache of the Embassy of the Republic of Austria in London, a very dear friend and a former Panzer Grenadier.

Acknowledgments

The authors would like to take this opportunity of thanking all those who have helped in the preparation of this book, and in particular Miss E. Austin, T. Charman, Mary Harris, Mr D. Henson, C. Hesse, L. Klein, Mrs Traude Lucas, Lt-Col Hubert Meyer, and Mr T. Shaw.

Our special thanks go to Alex Vanags-Baginskis for his care and help as editor.

The preparation of this book by two authors necessitated specialisation, and in order to explain variations in style, it is as well to indicate that James Lucas dealt with the four military operations, while Matthew Cooper was responsible for the chapters on the development, organisation and equipment.

Introduction

In wars of the past there was an axiom which is still true today, and which may still hold true in future non-atomic wars: that only infantry can hold captured ground. Guns, artillery, cavalry or tanks may destroy the main enemy opposition, but always the physical presence of the foot soldier was held to be essential to complete a military assault and to consolidate its success.

Following the invention of the tracked armoured fighting vehicle, the main and, indeed, principal role of the tank was seen to be tactical, in that it cleared the way for the follow-up infantry. This tied it to the pace of the foot soldier. Then came the revolutionary theory of armour being used strategically; a liberating concept which was to liberate it and to let it thrust forward in what have become known, erroneously, as 'Blitzkrieg' operations. But this theory raised the question: what happens to the tanks of the spearhead if there is no infantry back-up? Who would dominate the ground if the infantry had been left miles behind the armoured point unit? The obvious solution to this problem was to mount the infantry in tracked vehicles capable of cross country performance, which would then keep them forward with the armour; the two in contemporary military thought became a single entity.

The tank operating on its own was an inferior weapon, both in offence and defence, as some of Germany's enemies, with their 'all tank' theories found to their cost. The machine was, after all, an armoured, tracked weapon platform of large bulk and relative inflexibility; many were the places where its use was either restricted or impossible owing to the nature of the terrain, to the position of closely-built up areas or to the advent rain or snow. In such cases, infantry proved to be the one fighting arm capable of action. It was only when the tank was linked, within a single formation, to a sophisticated organisation of artillery, engineers, supply troops and, above all, mobile infantry, that it was able to operate effectively.

Thus, the tank was but a partner, albeit an important one, in a team of all arms known as the panzer (armoured) division, a team which achieved startling victories and maintained tenacious defence during the Second World War.

This book is concerned with the second main component of the German armoured division: the Panzer grenadiers. The title *Panzergrenadier* can be misleading; literally translated it means 'armoured

8

grenadier', thus implying that all those on whom it was bestowed were infantry mounted in tracked armoured personnel-carriers capable of withstanding enemy small-arms fire and of moving across most types of terrain in direct support of the tank. But this was never the case; the majority of 'Panzer grenadiers' were transported to battle only in untracked, unarmoured trucks, and were forced to fight, not necessarily in support, but often independently, of the tanks. It is, therefore, safer to translate *Panzergrenadier* as 'motorised infantry', for it was their mechanisation that set them apart from their foot-bound, horse-dependant, comrades of the ordinary infantry divisions. It was this that made them an elite, with higher selection requirements, better training, superior equipment levels, and the allocation of the most difficult of tasks, as the principal partners of the tank in war.

After 1943, Germany, lacking the potential for aggressive armoured warfare, was forced on the defensive, and thus there grew up the need for specialist infantry whose skill would compensate for the lack in numbers or of weapons. Having then nothing but a name and their courage, it was the Panzer Grenadiers who battled to hold the last position, who were flung, forlornly, to hold untenable lines or to achieve unrealisable objectives in still-born offensives. And those grenadiers of the last years of the war died without ever, or seldom, regaining the opportunity of serving strategically and of advancing behind an armoured spearhead into the positions of the enemy and there destroying him.

The successors of these German Panzer Grenadiers are to be found in all major contemporary armies irrespective of the name which they are given. These modern soldiers are the inheritors of those men whose stories are told here—the men who tried to realise the theory of armoured infantry in combat over 30 years ago.

Panzergrenadier was a title first used on 5 July 1942, and was applied to all infantry in panzer divisions; in March 1943 it was extended to cover the motorised infantry divisions as well. As the word did not mark the birth of any new arm, but merely altered the nomeclature of existing units, this study covers the history and evolution of the German motorised infantry from its conception in the 1930s to its final battles and capitulation in 1945. In many ways this work, the first on the subject in English, will be a companion volume to the authors' *PANZER: THE ARMOURED FORCE OF THE THIRD REICH*, also in this series, which deals with the theories, the successes and the failures of the German tank arm. However, this book is in no way dependent on the earlier one, and can be read without any reference to it. Here, the emphasis is placed on the motorised infantry, and an attempt made to provide some counter-weight to the hitherto unyielding dominance of the tank.

James Lucas
Matthew Cooper
                                                            London, 1977

A 4.7 cm self-propelled anti-tank gun on a PzKw I chassis in France, summer 1940. These were the first to be used by the motorised infantry but their open superstructure and high silhouette were considerable drawbacks.

The Development of Motorised Infantry

The 1920's and '30's witnessed a strong argument waged between European military leaders and theorists, one centred around the use of the tank in battle. It was a conflict of ideas and attitudes, and even of personalities, with many aspects, one of the most important of which being concerned with the new concept of motorised infantry. Were they to exist at all, and if so, in what numbers and in what form? Some, who composed a not inconsiderable body of opinion, saw little place for such formations, seeing the future of warfare to lie solely in the use of tanks. This was the 'all tank' theory, which maintained that modern inventions, especially the tank, but also the machine gun and improved fire-power generally, had rendered the infantryman useless; the soldier, 'naked' in his uniform and forced to carry heavy equipment, stood no chance on the battlefield, where bomb and bullet, together with a high standard of mobility, dominated. Tanks—tracked, armoured, gun platforms—were seen to be the only answer for the future. The modern army in offence was to be composed almost entirely of large tank formations capable of high mobility, fire power and protection; motorised infantry, who would be transported to battle, but forced to fight on foot, had no place in this.

Others, however, led by Sir Basil Liddell Hart in Great Britain (who advocated the idea of 'tank-marines') and by General Heinz Guderian in Germany, saw the importance of a closely-integrated team of all arms—tanks, infantry, artillery, engineers, reconnaissance troops—capable of producing the combination of maximum striking power, high speed across most terrains, and complete flexibility in response to enemy action, demanded by their concept of armoured warfare. Indeed, Guderian had arrived at an appreciation of the importance of motorised infantry before he had understood the potential of the tank. In 1922 he was posted to the Motorised Transport Department of the Inspectorate of Motorised Troops; of this, he later wrote: 'My work was certainly instructive, and what I learned in that office was to be useful to me later on. However, its principal value consisted in a study undertaken by General von Tschischwitz concerning the transport of troops by motorised vehicles. As a result of this study, which had been preceded by a small practical

The first panzer grenadiers —German infantrymen of the First World War collaborating with tanks in an attack

exercise. . . . I became for the first time aware of the possibility of employing motorised troops, and I was thus compelled to form my own opinions on this subject'.

From small acorns, large oaks grow; from motorised transport, Guderian was led to consider the use of the tank. He remembered: 'During the First World War there had been very many examples of the transport of troops by motorised vehicles. Such troop movements had always taken place behind a more or less static front line; they had never been used directly against the enemy in a war of movement. Germany now was undefended [her Army being limited by the Versailles Treaty to 100,000 men with neither tanks nor heavy artillery], and it therefore seemed impossible that any new war would start in the form of position warfare behind fixed fronts. We must rely on mobile defence in the case of war. The problem of the transport of motorised troops in mobile warfare soon raised the question of the protection of such transports. This could only satisfactorily be provided by armoured vehicles. I therefore looked for precedents from which I might learn about the experiments that had been made with armoured vehicles. This brought me in touch with Lieutenant Volckheim, who was then engaged in collating information concerning the very limited use of German armoured vehicles, and the incomparatively greater employment of enemy tank forces during the war, as a staff study for a little army'. Guderian was then introduced to works by the Englishmen, Fuller, Martel and Liddell Hart, in which the use of armoured forces predominated.

But Guderian was not obsessed by the tank to the exclusion of all else; motorised infantry remained an important part of his new theories. As he wrote: 'I learned from them [the Englishmen] the concentration of armour. . . . Further, it was Liddell Hart who emphasised the use of armour for long range strikes, operations against the opposing army's communications, and also proposed a type of armoured division combining panzer and panzer-infantry units. Deeply impressed with these ideas, I tried to develop them in a sense practicable for our own army'. At the same time, much interest was being shown throughout the German Army in the idea of motorised infantry used on their own, without tanks. One Lieutenant-Colonel von Brauchitsch, the future Commander-in-Chief of the German Army

Evolution of the panzer grenadier technique: Spanish Nationalist soldiers advancing behind a German PzKw I during the Spanish Civil War, 1938.

from 1938 to 1941, was particularly eminent in this field; in the winter of 1923–24, for example, he conducted manoeuvres to test the co-operation of motorised troops with aeroplanes. Many saw in the lorry and tracked vehicle a means by which the severe restrictions of horse transport could be overcome; the speed and distance of operations need no longer be dominated by the endurance of the foot soldier, or the limit to which a horse-drawn supply line could extend from the nearest rail-head (commonly believed to be only 50 miles). The motor engine gave the potential of hitherto unheard of freedom to operations; now, infantry could be taken over many miles to the very heart of the battle, before they were forced to dismount and fight on foot; all that was required was sufficient transport of the right type, an adequate supply of petrol, and an efficient repair service.

The specific tasks that were given to the motorised infantry developed from the early thoughts of the pioneers of armour. By the outbreak of war, these had been well-defined, and, after a few years of experimentation in battle, the basis of co-operation between panzer

Riflemen of a panzer division with their standard transport vehicle — a soft-skinned truck, entirely unsuited for the support of tanks.

General Guderian (on the right) in his command vehicle during the early stages of 'Operation Barbarossa'. The frame suspended overhead is an early type of radio antenna.

grenadiers and tanks was clear. This was laid down in many training manuals and pamphlets, and below is the official German Army view as given in HDv 967 (Field Service Regulations) dated 16 June 1944:

'The tank regiment, the heart of the panzer division, attacks the enemy as the spearhead of the attacking wedge ... and smashes them. Every other arm is dedicated to helping the tank advance and to use the fluid advance of the tanks to facilitate their own advance. Tanks cannot completely clear enemy from captured ground, and scattered groups of the enemy may combine to continue the fight.

'The panzer grenadier regiments follow the tanks in elongated echelon, and, collaborating with the second armoured wave, annihilate enemy remnants as well as carrying out the tasks of guarding and securing the rear and supply lines of the armoured units. Panzer grenadiers hold the areas captured by the tanks.

'Where a tank advance is obstructed by difficult terrain or by artificial barriers, the panzer grenadiers advance first. The conditions for this are: (a) attacking across rivers; (b) in heavily wooded areas, swamp or badly cut-up terrain; (c) mine-fields, anti-tank ditches and other tank obstacles; (d) when breaking through enemy anti-tank fronts. The tanks will give supporting fire to the panzer grenadiers' advance. Once past the obstacles, the tanks resume the leadership of the advance.

'This close co-operation between tanks and panzer grenadiers is often broken by local tactical situations; for example, heavy enemy resistance at the start of an assault, when combing through forests, in attacks and counterattacks and other crises. The stronger the enemy, and the more difficult the battle, the greater must be the attempts to increase this collaboration. Ground conditions affect the tanks, and the panzer grenadiers must follow the line of attack laid by the tanks.

'The points of similarity between the two arms of service depend upon the strengths and weaknesses of each. The weaknesses of one must be cancelled out by the strengths of the other.

Strengths of tanks	*Weaknesses of dismounted panzer grenadiers*
Protection against shrapnel	Unprotected
Morale effect upon the enemy	
Permanently ready to offer fire support.	Poorly equipped with armour-piercing weapons.
Speed of attack	No speed in attack.

Weaknesses of tanks	*Strengths of dismounted panzer grenadiers*
Deaf and partial blindness.	Hears and sees everything.
Susceptible to anti-tank and close-combat weapons.	
Large target unable to take immediate avoiding action.	Small target. Highly mobile.
Tank gun cannot be used from behind cover.	Has high angle weapons (e.g. mortars).
Dependent upon suitable terrain.	Can use and fight in any terrain.
Bad conditions restrict use.	

A self-propelled 2cm Flak 38 anti-aircraft gun used by panzer grenadiers.

'The following are basic regulations for collaboration: the tank fights the enemy tank and destroys the other weapons. The panzer grenadier looks out for hidden anti-tank guns and fires on them. He prevents close-quarter attack on the tanks. Covered by the tanks, he clears the enemy's position.

'Mutual assistance is essential.

'In good country the armour moves up by bounds from cover to cover, giving fire protection to the panzer grenadiers following. In wooded areas, the panzer grenadiers precede the tanks.

'When confronted with an anti-tank 'front', all tank guns are aimed at the enemy. . . . If ground conditions demand a frontal attack, the panzer grenadiers will begin one. Only when they have broken through and/or neutralised the anti-tank 'front' do the tanks go in.

'As tanks attract the mass of the enemy fire, the panzer grenadiers will dismount from the tank and take up assault-troop formation either behind or at the side of it, depending upon the ground.

'When with the support-wave tanks, or when there is no direct fire from the enemy, the panzer grenadiers can remain on the machines [tanks].

'Panzer grenadiers in armoured personnel-carriers follow behind the front wave. They destroy the enemy with the weapons they carry on their vehicles. When it is necessary to destroy armoured-piercing weapons, the panzer grenadiers will dismount from their carriers.

'Non-armoured panzer grenadiers can only ride into the assault if the enemy is not resisting, or is weak or shattered. The decision to attack by mounted or dismounted methods depends upon certain factors. The limited cross-country ability of the unarmoured panzer grenadiers restricts their use to good country or along roads.

'Tanks and panzer grenadiers in close combat will come under the same commander.
'When fighting in difficult and close country, it may be necessary to form [mixed] battle-groups.'

The ideal of a motorised infantry formation that developed in the early 1930's was summed up by General Lutz, the Head of the Armoured Troops Command, who wrote in 1936: 'The motorised infantry accompanying the tanks must be capable of going wherever the tanks can go. This, therefore, lays two conditions upon the motorised infantry: mobility and protection, both equal to that of the tanks. Tracked, armoured vehicles are an essential, for, without them, the accompanying infantry will not be able to keep up with the tanks

Panzer grenadiers during a training exercise. The officer-observer wears a white band around his cap to indicate that he is the 'umpire' of the wargames.

Motorised infantry during the attack on Poland. Note the Polish border marker in the back of the first truck.

across any terrain, or through shell and small-arms fire. Motorised infantry that cannot do this, lose much of their value.' But this ideal was to remain a dream forever. Indeed, for the majority of motorised infantry formations, the very opposite was to result, as was illustrated by the German Field Service Regulations, which stated: 'The lorries of the rifle brigade are a means of transport and are not fighting machines. The motorised infantry will debuss in the artillery belt and will make their way to the battlefield on foot, where they will serve as ordinary infantry.' Even at the height of the war, only one panzer grenadier battalion in ten could fulfill the dreams of men such as Guderian, Lutz and Liddell Hart.

The reasons for this lay in the scepticism prevalent within the German Army about the revolutionary principles that lay behind the employment of tanks and motorised infantry, and in the rapid rearmament which took place at Hitler's insistance before the outbreak of war in 1939, and which placed immense, almost unbearable, strains upon the Wehrmacht.

Hitler's Army, although a 20th century fighting machine, had its roots firmly embedded in its past. Dominated by a tradition extending back to the 1850's, the link that bound the Army to its history was strong enough to overcome the humiliation of defeat and the ravages of the peace treaties in 1918 and 1919. From two men, von Moltke and von Schlieffen, both former Chiefs of the General Staff, the Imperial German Army owed its principles of warfare, principles which placed emphasis upon fast, decisive manoeuvre aimed at the encirclement and the destruction of the mass of the enemy. Von Schlieffen coined the word *Vernichtungsgedanke*—the 'idea of annihilation'—the total destruction of the enemy's forces by means not of relatively slow, costly frontal attacks, but of swift, decisive blows from the flanks and the rear, all of

An aerial view of a panzer division on the attack in summer 1940. It shows the armoured spearhead, with riflemen in support.

One of the early types of assault guns during the first moments of the Western Campaign in May 1940

which were aimed at creating the decisive *Kesselschlachten*, 'cauldron battles', designed to surround, kill and capture the opposing army in as short a time as possible.

In the 1920's and 1930's, the method of warfare to be practiced by the German Army in the forthcoming decade was decided upon. The successors to von Moltke and von Schlieffen were the victors; the idea of *Vernichtungsgedanke* predominated, and Hitler's force was imbued with the belief in the power of the strategic initiative, manoeuvre, encirclement and annihilation. Infantry divisions, with their marching troops, horse-drawn guns and wagons, would remain the deciding factor of the strategy of decisive encirclement; the tanks and the motorised infantry would be subordinated to their needs. The new panzer formations would serve as the 'cutting edge' of the infantry's flanking thrusts; they would use their superior mobility and striking-power to break through the enemy's front-line, to rout his nearby reserves, to destroy his artillery positions, and, finally, to close the jaws of the pincer around the opposing forces. But the emphasis would still lie with the infantry, the means by which the iron ring round the enemy would be drawn tight, and his resistance overcome. As far as it

A motorcycle battalion moving through a French town in 1940.

An improvised self-propelled anti-tank gun: a 3.7 cm Pak 36 on a vehicle of a motorised infantry division in France, summer 1940.

went, this was all to the good, for the subsequent German victories were largely the result of a happy combination of traditional strategy and modern armament. But it did not go far enough. The senior generals failed to recognise that contemporary inventions may not just assist traditional warfare, they might revolutionise it.

The revolutionaries, led by Liddel Hart in Great Britain and by Guderian in Germany, did not fail to understand that they had within their grasp the potential to alter warfare out of all recognition. These men evolved a new mobile strategy of revolutionary proportions from the tactics of infiltration, based upon the principles of surprise, speed in attack, and the penetration of the enemy's 'nerve centres' (his headquarters and lines of communications), which were used to such effect by the Germans in the last year of the First World War, and from the introduction of the lorry, the armoured tracked vehicle and the aeroplane, which, as has been indicated above, gave a large measure of independence to the armies in the field from the restrictions of supply and the limitations of the speed and endurance of horses and men on foot. Owing to the emphasis they placed upon mobility and armour, their concept may be called the 'armoured idea'. Certainly, this strategy had certain superficial similarities with *Vernichtungsgedanke*—decisive manoeuvre was common to both—but in essence the two found themselves in direct conflict. The physical destruction of the enemy was supplanted by the paralysis of his command as the first objective; well co-ordinated encirclements were replaced by un-supported thrusts deep into the enemy's rear; flank protection and secure supply lines gave way to velocity and unpredictability as the basic rules of operation; centralised control was superceded by independence of action; and the large infantry-dominated armies made way for the small, untried armoured force as the main instrument of victory. This novel idea of strategy was too revolutionary to be accepted by the leadership of the German Army, and it was, therefore, never to be translated into reality.

A 3.7 cm Pak 36 anti-tank gun and an assault gun on a Panzer IV chassis during the invasion of the Soviet Union in summer 1941.

One of the most important results was that the mechanised arm, composed of tanks and motorised infantry, on which Guderian and others based all their hopes for victory, was always to be neglected and misused, its potential disregarded in favour of the established, traditional strategy of decisive manoeuvre, in which the marching infantry predominated.

Thus, the arguments and activities of men such as Guderian met with considerable opposition. As General von Thoma remembered: '... the development of armoured forces met with much resistance from the higher generals of the German Army. ... The older ones were afraid of developing such forces fast—because they themselves did not understand the technique of armoured warfare, and were uncomfortable with such new instruments. At the best they were interested, but dubious and cautious. We could have gone ahead much faster but for their attitude'. Guderian called the Chief of the Army General Staff, Beck, a 'paralysing element wherever he appeared', and dismissed his successor, Halder, as a 'gentleman of the horse-artillery'. They, for their part, viewed him as a 'hothead', and regarded his ideas as those of a 'technician' without much grounding in reality. Guderian noted that 'there were many heated discussions of the problem [of mechanisation] and more sceptics than believers in the possibility of finding a solution'. The number of vehicles required was daunting, and caused considerable concern to those who had to translate theory into reality. To many officers, the new ideas were unsettling. Guderian records an early incident which exemplifies this attitude: '... I expressed the hope that, as a result of our efforts, we were on the way to transforming our motorised units from supply troops into combat troops. My Inspector [von Natzmer], however, held a contrary opinion, and informed me bluntly: "To hell with combat! They're supposed to carry flour!" And that was that!'

Almost as damaging to the future of the German mechanised force was the rushed expansion of the German Army between the years 1933 and 1939. Despite the warnings of the generals, Hitler insisted on building up the size of his armed forces as quickly as possible, regardless of quality. To him, numbers spelt power. In 1933, the German Army contained 100,000 men devoid of tanks and heavy artillery; by the middle of 1939, just two months before the outbreak of the European War, it numbered no less than 730,000 men, with a further 1,100,000 in reserve; upon mobilisation, over 3,700,000 men would be under arms. These figures represent a 500 per cent increase in active formations in only six years, and a 1000 per cent increase in total mobilised strength. In just seven years, a force 18 times the size of the original body had been trained and equipped. It was a startling performance. But quality inevitably suffered; a number of generals were convinced that standards had sunk so low that the German Army had become a 'blunt sword'. Most important of all for the mechanised force, was that the huge strains imposed upon the armament industry of the Reich, together with the extreme cost to the government of rearmament, meant that the proper equipping of the few armoured and motorised units that were raised was an impossibility. Scarce equipment, especially tracked vehicles, were dissipated throughout the Army. As Guderian wrote: 'The development of tracked vehicles for the tank-supporting arms never went as fast as we wished. It was clear that the effectiveness of the tanks would gain in proportion to the ability of the infantry, artillery and other divisional arms to follow them in an advance across country. We wanted lightly-armed half-tracks for the riflemen, combat engineers and medical services, armoured self-propelled guns for the artillery and the anti-tank battalions, and various types of armour for the reconnaissance and signals battalions. The equipment of the divisions with these vehicles was never fully completed.' In 1939, of the 2,060-odd motor vehicles in a panzer division, not one was wholly tracked, few were half-tracked, and only one type was armoured—the SdKfz 251 half-track personnel carrier, and this was found only extremely rarely. By the outbreak of war, less than one fifth of all vehicles in the panzer division possessed a cross-country mobility approaching that of the tanks. Road-bound, unarmoured trucks did not lend themselves to the full exploitation of armoured warfare, and yet with these all but a few units of motorised infantry went to war; of the nearly 400 companies in September 1939, just two or three were tracked and armoured.

It is against this background that the development of the German mechanised force in general, and the panzer grenadiers in particular, must be viewed. Nor did the outbreak of war do much to enhance Guderian's ideal. The deficiencies, with which the motorised infantry had entered the field, could never be made good in the face of huge losses, further expansion, relatively low production, and continued neglect. Thus, in May 1940, when the invasion of the West began, it appears that of the 80 battalions of motorised infantry then in existence, only two were 'armoured'—that is, equipped with the SdKfz 251. In June 1941, as the German armies invaded the Soviet Union, the position was little better, and only very few companies among the 185 battalions of riflemen were afforded the mobility and protection they required. By September 1943, when the equipping of the panzer

Elite motorised infantry during a victory parade—men of the Leibstandarte SS 'Adolf Hitler' *in 1940.*

grenadiers was at its height, of the 226 battalions to be found in the panzer and panzer grenadier divisions of the Army, the Luftwaffe and the Waffen-SS, only 26 were classed as 'armoured'.

However, despite this frustration of the panzer grenadier ideal, the importance of the German motorised infantry did not diminish, but grew with the passage of time. At the beginning of the war, the role of the motorised infantry was strictly subordinate to that of the tank. This was revealed by the German Field Service Regulations, which defined their tasks as: 'To clean up the break-through area and to break down any remaining enemy resistance; to defend the ground taken; to attack the enemy's flank and rear so as to enlarge the break-through area; to protect the flanks and rear of own units against enemy counterattacks'. By the end of the war, however, a memorandum prepared by the German Army High Command said: 'There can be no doubt that, without the closest co-operation of the panzer grenadier with the tank, the latter is of limited value in the conditions under which they are forced to fight. It is even said by some that commanders would prefer to lose tanks rather that their infantry carriers'.

The reasons for this transformation were three; the realisation that close co-operation between tank and panzer grenadier was essential; the changing nature of warfare from the wide-ranging sweeps, in which the power and mobility of the tank excelled, to the closely-fought battles of attrition, in which the physical possession of ground became paramount; and the depletion of the tank force as the result of Hitler's

An armoured phalanx on the move. Tanks and personnel carriers during the early stages of 'Operation Barbarossa' in summer 1941.

desire for expansion, the relatively limited output of new machines from the Reich's factories, and the high losses caused by enemy action or breakdown.

In 1935, the year in which the first three armoured formations were raised, the offensive capacity of the panzer division rested firmly upon its two tank regiments, which, between them, possessed some 560 tanks. The motorised infantry were very much regarded as their supporters, and comprised one, 2-battalion rifle regiment and a motor cycle battalion grouped in a brigade. However, manoeuvres soon revealed that there existed a poor balance between the tanks and the infantry, and the rifle regiment was therefore given an extra two battalions; the new panzer divisions that were raised were each given two, 2-battalion rifle regiments, an organisation that was soon to become standard for all armoured formations. An increase in infantry strength was soon to be accompanied by a decrease in tank strength. The numbers of tanks in each company were reduced by 10, so that the total machines in the division fell to 400; upon mobilisation in August 1939, after one in four of the companies were removed from each division to form depot and replacement units, the total of tanks in a division was 328. But worse was to come. After the Polish campaign, three of the four new panzer divisions were given only 240 tanks, while the other received even less: 160. This latter figure was soon to become standard; after the French campaign, Hitler decided upon the doubling of the number of his panzer divisions, to be effected by the simple expedient of halving the tank strength of the individual divisions. Thus, the armoured divisions which invaded the Soviet Union in June 1941 consisted of one tank regiment of two battalions with 160 tanks (six divisions had three battalions), and four battalions

24

Tanks and armoured personnel carriers advance in mixed formation in South Russia, 1942. Note the flat countryside offering little cover to vehicles and men.

of motorised infantry, as well as a motor-cycle battalion. A complete reversal of the original ratio of tank to infantry had been brought about.

In 1942, there were attempts to reverse this process, and the motor-cycle battalion was removed from the order of battle of the panzer division. At the same time, the number of companies in each tank battalion increased from three to the original four. However, there were simply not enough tanks available, and the nominal establishment of 200 machines in each division was hardly ever reached; half that number, or less, was the usual battle-strength for army formations. By further reorganisations of establishments in 1944 and 1945, the nominal number of tanks in a panzer division was brought down to 120 by the beginning of 1945. And all the while that this was going on, the panzer grenadiers were becoming more essential to the panzer division. Although there were no further increases in personnel strength, heavier weapons were provided, and a formidable fire-power was built up to compensate for the shortage of tanks. Thus, in 1939, the three battalions of riflemen and the battalion of motor cycle troops between them possessed 110 light and 56 heavy machine-guns, 36 light and 24 medium mortars, 8 light infantry guns, and 12 x 3.7 cm anti-tank guns; in 1944, the four battalions of panzer grenadiers had 364 light and 49 heavy machine guns, no light but 28 medium and 16 heavy mortars, no light but 12 heavy infantry guns, 40 x 2 cm anti-aircraft guns and 12 x 7.5 cm guns. The anti-tank guns had been given over to panzer division's anti-tank battalion (which possessed 43 x 7.5 cm anti-tank guns), but it always worked in close co-operation with the panzer grenadiers.

The increasing importance of the panzer grenadiers within the panzer division was revealed also in the reliance placed upon the *Kampfgruppe*—'Battle Group'. This began in late 1941 and early 1942, when, in order to form a strong, mobile attacking force that was not too large to be unwieldy, one armoured panzer grenadier battalion, one artillery battalion and one tank battalion were organised as a separate entity within the division. So successful was the experiment, that the following years saw an extension of its use. In 1943, orders went out to concentrate the best elements of the division into these 'battle-groups' for the purposes of attack or counter-attack, and tables of organisation were laid down. A *Panzerkampfgruppe*, as it was then called, was to consist of one tank battalion of 40 to 60 tanks, one armoured panzer grenadier battalion (the only one in the division) of 50 to 80 medium personnel carriers, one armoured artillery battalion, usually of the batteries of *Wespe* self-propelled 10.5 cm guns, and one armoured pioneer company. With the help of the armoured reconnaissance battalion, a panzer division could sometimes form a second battle-group, although lacking an artillery battalion that was armoured.

The battle group was, clearly, well-tailored to the needs of the German Army in the latter half of the war. Shortage of tanks, and the increased role played by the panzer grenadiers, made such a grouping almost inevitable, and the nature of the defensive fighting from 1942 to 1945 made it also highly desirable. Quick, powerful counter-attacks to stem enemy break-throughs were required of Germany's armoured arm, and this, the panzer battle group, with its equality between tank, infantry and artillery, and its emphasis upon mobility, protection and

Riflemen moving up in support of a self-propelled 5 cm anti-tank gun. Eastern Front, summer 1941.

Motorised German riflemen in the Western Desert aboard a captured British 15 cwt truck. At one time no less than 85 per cent of German transport in North Africa consisted of captured vehicles.

A group of SdKfz 251's move into attack across the flat Russian countryside, 1943.

After closing in aboard their armoured SdKfz 251 carrier, panzer grenadiers go into action against an enemy position. Eastern Front, summer 1941.

fire-power, was able to provide. In March 1945, the final stage in the recognition of the panzer grenadier as an equal partner with the tank came in the reorganisation of the armoured divisions. Based upon the idea of the battle group, the panzer division in 1945 consisted of one tank battalion of 54 tanks, one self-propelled anti-tank gun battalion, one armoured panzer grenadier battalion and four motorised panzer grenadier battalions. The tank regiment now consisted of one tank battalion and one armoured panzer grenadier battalion. Equality had arrived.

The increasing importance of the panzer grenadier was also revealed by the development of the motorised infantry divisions. The first four were raised in 1937, and consisted of three, 4-battalion motorised infantry regiments supported by artillery, reconnaissance, engineer and service units. After the campaign in Poland, each regiment was reduced by one battalion, the 4-battalion structure having been found too unwieldly in action.· However, the Army High Command believed that the divisions, although mounted entirely in un-armoured trucks, had proved themselves to be extremely useful (together with the panzer divisions, they had spearheaded the attacking armies with considerable success), and by 1941 their number had more than doubled to 13 (of which 3 belonged to the Waffen-SS), together with 2 brigades (one Waffen-SS), and 2 strong infantry regiments (one Waffen-SS). At the peak of the war, in late 1943, there were no less than 23 panzer grenadier divisions in the field, 12 of the Army and 11

Riflemen in the attack. Soviet Union, summer 1941.

of the Waffen-SS (of the latter, seven were soon to be renamed panzer divisions; one of the Army's also possessed the strength of an armoured formation.)

The first campaign in the Soviet Union in 1941 had revealed the value of motorised infantry working in close co-operation with armour (indeed, the Army's elite motorised infantry regiment, *Grossdeutschland*, possessed within its order of battle an assault-gun company which had proved extremely effective); therefore, for the forthcoming 1942 summer offensive in the south of Russia, the German High Command resolved to provide each of the motorised infantry divisions within the attacking force with one battalion of tanks (45 machines in total), mainly PzKw III's. By mid-1943, this new organisation had become standard for all, the only variation being that, because of the acute shortage of battle-worthy tanks, assault-guns were put to increasing use as the war progressed. The 1944-model panzer grenadier division was provided with an armoured battalion with 42 assault-guns or tanks. The Luftwaffe and Waffen-SS panzer grenadier divisions, with the exception of those raised after 1942, had considerably higher tank and assault-gun strengths than their Army counterparts, and at least four of them, 1st SS, 2nd SS, 3rd SS and *Hermann Göring*, were strong panzer divisions in all but name. The Army Panzer Grenadier Division *Grossdeutschland* possessed the highest tank strength of all; at the battle of Kursk in July 1943, for example, it had 163 tanks and 35 assault-guns, while the Waffen-SS 1st, 2nd, and 3rd divisions averaged 131 and 35 respectively (it should be noted that the Army panzer divisions each had an average of only 73 tanks).

Motorised infantry lifting mines during an advance.

However, although the panzer grenadier divisions grew in importance during the war (the reliance placed upon them as the 'fire-brigade' of Germany's defences was almost as great as that upon the panzer divisions), and despite the fact that they were equipped with armoured vehicles, their troops remained mounted in trucks. Only *Grossdeutschland* was equipped with armoured personnel carriers, and then only one battalion's worth. Thus, at the beginning of October 1943, of the 130 panzer grenadier battalions in the Army and Waffen-SS panzer grenadier divisions, only 3 were armoured (two of them from the Waffen-SS). Such was the result of the severe shortages in the equipment of the German Army.

Organisation

On the 15 October 1935, the first three panzer divisions were formed, the genesis of a force which was to approach 40 divisions at its height. Three *Schützen* (Rifle) Regiments were raised, each of two battalions, and distributed, singly, to the armoured divisions, as were three independent motorcycle battalions. The offensive power of a panzer division was divided between two tank regiments grouped into a brigade and one rifle regiment and one motorcycle battalion, also grouped into a brigade. However, the correct balance between tank and rifleman was not yet deemed to have been arrived at. In November 1938, the 5th Panzer Division was given two rifle regiments, each of two battalions; this was soon to become the standard organisation for the future.

At the same time as the fifth panzer division was being raised, four new formations were being added to the German Army; these were Light Divisions, which came under the control of the Inspector of Cavalry, and were regarded as mechanised cavalry divisions with a 'stiffener' of tanks. Instead of the four tank battalions of the panzer divisions, the light divisions had just one, but were given either three or four battalions of cavalry riflemen to form their main attacking force.

The organisation of a panzer division rifle regiment at the outbreak of war was as follows:

Panzer Divisions 1, 2, and 3:

Headquarters
2 Rifle Battalions, each of
    2 Rifle Companies
    1 Motorcycle Company
    1 Machine-gun Company
    1 Heavy Company (anti-tank, infantry-gun and pioneer platoons)
    1 Light Infantry Column

A total of 2,203 men (58 officers), 54 light machine-guns, 28 heavy machine-guns, 18 light and 12 medium mortars, 6 x 3.7 cm anti-tank guns, and 4 light infantry-guns.

Riflemen manhandling a 2 cm Flak 38 anti-aircraft gun into position during the invasion of France in summer 1940. The white initial 'G' on the back of the truck denotes that they belonged to Cen. Guderian's command.

Panzer Divisions 4 and 5:

As above, except lacking a machine-gun battalion and a light infantry battalion; the heavy company was organised differently, with 1 anti-tank gun, 1 mortar, and 2 infantry-gun platoons. Weapon allocations were higher.

A total of 2,260 men (61 officers), 108 light and 24 heavy machine-guns, 18 light and 12 heavy mortars, 6 x 3.7 cm anti-tank guns and 8 light infantry-guns.

Panzer Division 5 had two such regiments.

The motorcycle battalion was organised as follows:
Headquarters
    3 Motorcycle Companies
    1 Machine-gun Company
    1 Heavy Company (anti-tank, infantry-gun and pioneer platoons)
A total of 957 men (26 officers), 27 light and 14 heavy machine-guns, 9 light and 6 heavy mortars, 3 x 3.7 cm anti-tank guns and 2 infantry-guns.

After the campaign in Poland, the light divisions were reformed into panzer divisions; at the same time, the other panzer divisions were reinforced, either by a further battalion of riflemen or by a whole regiment. There were then no less than five different types of rifle brigade within the panzer divisions.

In 1941, came the massive expansion of the panzer arm ordered the year before. The basic organisation of the rifle regiment now came to be based on two battalions, each of 3 rifle companies, one machine-gun company and one heavy company, while each division possessed two such regiments and a motorcycle battalion within the rifle brigade. In the summer of 1942, when the title 'Panzergrenadier' was first used, the brigade grouping was disbanded and the motorcycle battalion incorporated within the reconnaissance detachment of the division; at the time that this took place, the rifle brigade was composed of 4,443 men (139 officers) with 300 light and 48 heavy machine-guns, 24 medium mortars, 9 x 2.8 cm, 9 x 3.7 cm and 18 x 5 cm anti-tank guns, 36 anti-tank rifles, 16 light and 8 heavy infantry-guns. The standard organisation included an armoured rifle battalion equipped with SdKfz 251s, and the motorcycle company equipped with SdKfz 250s.

By mid-1943, the general rule was that one of the two panzer grenadier regiments within a panzer division was classified as 'armoured'—that is to say, it had one of its two battalions mounted in armoured personnel carriers. The organisation of the two regiments, as laid down in September 1943, was as follows:

An SdKfz 251, with its personnel dismounted guarding a cross-roads on the Eastern Front, summer 1941.

Panzer Grenadier Regiment (armoured)

Headquarters (accompanied by motorcycle, signals, pioneer, heavy anti-tank gun platoons)
1 Panzer Grenadier Battalion (armoured) with three panzer grenadier companies and one heavy company
1 Panzer Grenadier Battalion (motorised) organised as above
1 Anti-aircraft Company (self-propelled)
1 Heavy Infantry-gun Company (self-propelled)
1 Pioneer Company (one platoon of which was armoured)

Panzer Grenadier Regiment (motorised)

Was organised as above, with the following exceptions: a motorised battalion instead of the armoured; the anti-aircraft company was towed, and the pioneer company did not possess an armoured platoon.

Between them, the two regiments had a total of 305 light and 77 heavy machine-guns, 36 medium mortars, 15 x 7.5 cm anti-tank guns, 2 light and 12 heavy infantry guns, 42 flamethrowers, 1 x 2 cm and 9 x 3.7 cm cannon, and 24 x 2 cm anti-aircraft guns. This represented a significant increase in the fire-power of the panzer grenadiers. In the autumn of 1943, of 47 panzer grenadier regiments and 92 battalions within the panzer divisions, 21 regiments and 21 battalions respectively were called 'armoured'. Of the 963 vehicles within the two regiments, only 120 were tracked and armoured—the SdKfz 251s.

However, the theoretical tables of organisation were not compatable with the realities of war; as a result of high losses and relatively low production, the panzer grenadiers were seldom up to full strength.

Panzer grenadiers combing the area for Soviet troops in summer 1941. Here they have just captured a straggler.

Riflemen of Genral Guderian's Panzer Group (identified by the white 'G' on their SdKfz 251's) on the move in Central Russia, 1941.

Battalions often shrank from 1,000 men to 100, and equipment levels remained low. There were many variations on the basic organisation as laid down by the Army High Command; for example, well over half the infantry-gun companies were not self-propelled, and only 18 of the 47 regiments possessed anti-aircraft companies. Only the *Panzer Lehr Division*, formed in November 1943, had all four panzer grenadier battalions mounted in SdKfz 251s.

The 1944 organisation, introduced in September of that year, contained a number of changes; the anti-tank guns were given over to the division's anti-tank battalion, the anti-aircraft company was disbanded and its guns distributed within the regiments, and supply company was added to each battalion. The armoured panzer grenadier regiment had a personnel complement of 2,264 (56 officers), most of them mounted in 120 SdKfz 251s, and the motorised, 2,167 (49 officers).

In March 1945, a completely new organisation for the panzer division was introduced, and panzer grenadiers assumed a dominant role. The tank regiment was composed of one tank battalion and one armoured panzer grenadier battalion (headquarters, 3 panzer grenadier companies and one supply company). The panzer division also included two motorised panzer grenadier regiments, organised along previous lines, with the addition of one heavy machine-gun company for each battalion. Between them, the five panzer grenadier battalions had 199 light and 32 heavy machine-guns, 12 medium and 16 heavy mortars, 33 x 2 cm anti-aircraft guns, 8 heavy infantry-guns, 6 x 7.5 cm anti-tank guns, and 81 anti-tank rocket launchers.

The Waffen-SS panzer divisions had panzer grenadier regiments similar to those of the Army, with the following differences: as a legacy from their days as panzer grenadier divisions, each regiment had three instead of two battalions (over 3,000 men); and, as a result of their favoured position in the eyes of the Führer, they had better equipment levels. This meant that, by the end of 1944, every one of their panzer grenadier regiments was classified as 'armoured' (in other words, one of the three battalions in every regiment was provided with SdKfz 251s). The Luftwaffe division *Hermann Göring* had its panzer grenadier regiments organised like those of the Army. Both in the Air Force and the SS formations, an assault gun battalion was incorporated, also as a legacy from their past as panzer grenadier divisions.

Panzer Grenadier Divisions

At the outbreak of war, the motorised infantry division was exactly what its name suggested: it was an infantry division that had been mounted in trucks rather than being made dependant upon the feet of its soldiers and the endurance of horses. Its later role as an armoured formation was yet to come. Thus, the motorised infantry division was

A SdKfz 251 with its full complement of personnel during the 1942 summer campaign in the southern USSR.

A 'tank hunter' on a training ground in Germany, 1942: modified PzKw II chassis fitted with a 7.5 cm Pak.

Panzer grenadiers receiving orders during the battle of Kursk, July 1943.

A 'Hummel' 15 cm self-propelled gun, one of the heavy support weapons used in panzer grenadier divisions.

organised exactly as was its counterpart in the first line of ordinary infantry formations. It was composed as follows:

Headquarters
3 Regiments of 3 battalions each
1 Reconnaissance Battalion
1 Artillery Regiment
1 Anti-tank Battalion
1 Pioneer Battalion
1 Signals Battalion
Supply services etc.

The total of men in the division was 16,445 (492 officers) equipped with 989 troop trucks, 1,687 other trucks, 1,323 motorcycles, 621 motorcycle combinations, 30 armoured cars, 374 light and 130 heavy machine-guns, 84 light and 54 heavy mortars, 24 light infantry guns, 72 x 3.7 cm anti-tank guns, 36 light and 12 heavy field howitzers, and 12 x 2 cm anti-aircraft guns.

After the value of the motorised infantry divisions had been proved in Poland, some attempt was made to adapt them fully to the demands of modern mobile warfare, and one of the infantry regiments was taken from each division so as to make the latter more easy to handle when moving fast. Thereafter, the organisation of the motorised infantry division remained unchanged until the summer of 1942, when a number of them were provided with a battalion of tanks; within a relatively short time this was to become standard. In September 1943, the Army High Command laid down the following organisation for the

Rifleman practising close combat attack techniques with explosive charges. The tanks is a captured French Hotchkiss H 39/40.

A battle group of Waffen-SS panzer grenadiers during the defensive fighting in the East in autumn 1944. Like infantry, they are wearing the reversible thick field grey/white autumn-winter camouflage suits.

panzer grenadier divisions (as they had become known in March, although not all of their regiments were so called, some retaining their former titles of *Grenadier* or *Fusilier*):

Headquarters
2 Regiments, each with 3 battalions, infantry-gun, anti-aircraft and
    pioneer companies
1 Tank or Assault-gun Battalion
1 Reconnaissance Battalion
1 Anti-tank Battalion (self-propelled)
1 Artillery Regiment
1 Anti-aircraft Battalion
1 Pioneer Battalion
1 Signals Battalion
Suppy units etc.

The division was composed of 15,418 men (415 officers), 685 light and 98 heavy machine-guns, 46 medium and 24 heavy mortars, 14 light and 4 heavy infantry guns, 21 heavy anti-tank guns, 42 x 2 cm and 8 x 8.8 cm anti-aircraft guns, 24 flame-throwers, 24 light and 8 heavy field howitzers, 4 x 10 cm cannon, 18 armoured cars, 43 self-propelled anti-tank guns, and 45 tanks or assault-guns. Because of the severe shortages then being suffered by the panzer formations, it was not too unusual for a full-strength panzer grenadier division to possess as much armour as a depleted panzer division.

In 1944, a new organisation was introduced; although the number of personnel dropped by some 680 men, the increase of weaponry continued (with the exception of armour), so that, for example, the division possessed an extra 50 light and 8 heavy machine-guns and 4 x 8.8 cm anti-aircraft guns. Any remaining tanks gave way to assault-guns. However, still there was no introduction of the armoured personnel carrier, and the panzer grenadier division of 1944 had only 7 within its order of battle (the panzer division had 287). Till the end, the truck remained the standard transport for the panzer grenadier. In the March 1945 reorganisation, the panzer grenadier division as a separate entity ceased to exist; all became panzer divisions.

The *Grossdeutschland* and *Feldherrnhalle* panzer grenadier divisions were organised differently from the rest: *Grossdeutschland* had no less than four tank and one assault-gun battalions, while *Feldherrnhalle* had four companies instead of three in each panzer grenadier battalion. The Waffen-SS panzer grenadier divisions, Nos. 1, 2, 3, and 5, were also well equipped with armour, having one regiment of tanks and one battalion of assault guns, which, in effect, made them strong panzer divisions.

Equipment

Mobility, flexibility and fire-power were the key factors in the organisation and equipment of the German motorised infantry. In the mobile warfare of the Second World War, each was indispensable to the others, and none can be relegated to a secondary role. Without full mobility, the panzer grenadiers could not keep pace with the tanks, or act independently with success; without proper flexibility, they could not react instantly to the new situations that would constantly arise on the battle field; and without adequate fire-power, they would be unable to defeat the enemy upon their meeting.

However, the panzer grenadiers were never to be well equipped for their role. Tracked armoured vehicles were essential, but were nevertheless a rarity. Out of four battalions of riflemen in a panzer division, only one was provided with the SdKfz 251 armoured personnel carrier, and this was not until late 1942; and few indeed were the panzer grenadier divisions that could mount any of its infantry in such vehicles. The artillery regiments of panzer grenadier divisions were similarly ill-provided for, not until 1943 were some of their guns put onto self-propelled mounts, and then their superstructures were open-topped and their crews susceptible to shell splinters.

Of all their weapons, the armoured personnel carrier and the assault-gun may be said to typify the panzer grenadiers; others they shared with the rest of the Army (although it must not be thought that the armoured personnel carrier and the assault-gun were exclusive to the panzer grenadiers), such as infantry small arms, artillery, anti-tank guns, and armoured cars.

Medium Armoured Personnel Carrier

The SdKfz 251 half-tracked personnel carrier is generally regarded to be the vehicle typifying the *Panzergrenadier*. But able and advanced machine though it was, well-suited to the demanding conditions of armoured warfare, the SdKfz 251 was more the exception than the rule among German motorised infantry formations. As stated before, the idea of all motorised infantry riding into battle immune from small arms fire and shell splinters, and independent of the limitations imposed by adherence to a road system, remained a dream for all but a relatively few formations.

In 1933, the Army Ordnance Office placed an order with Hansa-Lloyd-Goliath works of Bremen for a half-track tractor capable of towing loads of up to three tons, the prototype of which emerged the next year. A number of versions followed, the final one, designated type 'H kl 6' being introduced in 1938, and remaining in production until 1944. It was from this vehicle that the standard German armoured personnel carrier of the Second World War was to emerge.

The need for some type of infantry carrier that was well-armoured, tracked and properly armed, to be used in place of the soft-skinned, four-wheeled, unarmed truck, was never explicitly recognised by the Army authorities. Not until 1938 was the Ordnance Office to present specifications for a special infantry vehicle, and then it was far from ideal. Guderian had wanted a completely new fighting machine, from which it was possible for infantry to fight while on the move if necessary; instead, the armoured force was presented with a lightly-armoured carrier intended only to transport troops onto the battlefield, where they would dismount and fight on foot. The Hanomag Company of Hanover, under the instruction of the Army Ordnance Office, took the standard three-ton half-tracked tractor chassis, to which it made some minor modifications, and on it placed an open-topped superstructure with an armour thickness of only 12 mm at the front and 8 mm on its sides. The vehicle was capable of holding 12 men, including the driver. Thus was born the standard *Gepanzerter Mannschafts-Transportwagen* (armoured personnel carrier) to be used by the German Wehrmacht.

Riflemen practising dismounting from an SdKfz 251 in late 1939; this is one of the first vehicles of this type issued to the Field Army.

41

A column of SdKfz 251 armoured personnel carriers during the early stages of 'Operation Barbarossa'. The draped flag was used for ground-to-air identification purposes.

Panzer grenadiers having a hurried meal while aboard their armoured personnel carriers. Soviet Union, 1941.

An SdKfz 251/8 armoured ambulance of the
'Grossdeutschland' division. These vehicles
could accommodate either four stretcher cases or
up to ten lightly wounded troops.

Internal view of an SdKfz 250/3 radio
communication vehicle. Note the MG 42 with
carrying straps stowed opposite the radio set.

The first prototype emerged in late 1938, and, after trials, was accepted by the Ordnance Office, which gave to it the designation SdKfz 251 *mittlerer* (Medium) *gepanzerter Mannschaftskraftwagen,* and the first service issue came in the spring of 1939. By the next year, the basic models, *Ausführung* (Model) *A, B,* and *C* had appeared, possessing only minor differences between them. In 1942, the SdKfz 251 was retitled *mittlerer Schützenpanzerwagen* (mSPW-Riflemen's armoured vehicle). In 1943, *Ausführung D* appeared, its considerably modified superstructure—with a squared-off body and more internal capacity—designed to facilitate ease of mass production rather that to advance any new technical development. The overall effect was to give the SdKfz 251 a cleaner, streamlined shape to its superstructure, which involved a halving of the number of separate armoured plates hitherto required in its manfacture.

The SdKfz 251 had a length of 19 ft. (19 ft. 7 ins. for *Ausf.D*), a height of 6 ft. 11 ins. and a width of 6 ft. 11 ins. With a battle-weight of 8.8 tons, and carrying 12 men (commander, driver and 10 men—one squad), it was capable of a maximum road speed of 32 mph. Its speed across country was 26 mph. Armament consisted of two machine guns, and two sub-machine-guns. Armour thickness was increased to 14.5 mm for the front, but remained 8 mm on the sides. Of special interest were the tracks, which were of unique and sophisiticated construction, and fairly reliable.

The SdKfz 251 was highly versatile—perhaps its greatest strength—and by the end of the war there had been no less than 22 variants in service. They were:

SdKfz 251/1   medium armoured personnel carrier—as above.

SdKfz 251/2   medium 81 mm mortar carrier, with crew of 8 and
                   one machine-gun.

Late production versions of the SdKfz 251 featured more streamlined superstructure.

SdKfz 251/3	wireless command vehicle in five versions with crew of 7, and one machine-gun.
SdKfz 251/4	towed the light 7.5 cm infantry howitzer, and carried its ammunition, with a crew of 7 and one machine-gun; no longer in production by 1944.
SdKfz 251/5	engineer vehicle with specialised equipment, a crew of 8 and two machine-guns.
SdKfz 251/6	command vehicle for general staff officers.
SdKfz 251/7 I and II	two versions of an engineer vehicle, with crew of 8 and two machine-guns.
SdKfz 251/8 I and II	armoured ambulance, with a crew of 2 and capable of carrying 4 stretchers or 10 lightly injured men.
SdKfz 251/9	equipped with a 7.5 cm KwK L/24 (AFV cannon), and with a crew of 3.
SdKfz 251/10	equipped with a 3.7 cm Pak (anti-tank gun) with a crew of 6. It was a platoon leader's vehicle; from 1942 some were equipped with the 2.8 cm tapered-bore Pak. No longer in production by 1944.
SdKfz 251/11	telephone cable vehicle with a crew of 5
SdKfz 251/12	artillery survey section instrument carrier.
SdKfz 251/13	artillery sound-recording vehicle.
SdKfz 251/14	artillery sound-ranging vehicle.
SdKfz 251/15	artillery flash-spotting vehicle.
SdKfz 251/16	flamethrower, with two 14 mm flamethrowers, one 7 mm flamethrower, and one machine-gun.

Field maintenance work on an SdKfz 251/9 armed with a 7.5 cm gun used in support role during the battle of Kursk in July 1943.

SdKfz 251/17 — equipped with a 2 cm Flak 38 (anti-aircraft gun), with a crew of 3 and a machine-gun.

SdKfz 251/18 — observation post vehicle.

SdKfz 251/19 — used as a telephone exchange.

SdKfz 251/20 — support vehicle for Panther tanks. Equipped with a large infra-red searchlight for night operations.

SdKfz 251/21 — a replacement for SdKfz 251/17 in 1944.

SdKfz 251/22 — equipped with a 7.5 cm Pak 40 L/48.

Medium armoured personnel carrier SdKfz 251
Details (basic model)

Crew	12 men (driver, section leader, 10 panzer grenadiers)
Armament	2 x 7.92 mm MG 34 or 42; 2 sub-machine guns, 6-8 rifles
Armour	Front—14.5 mm, side—8 mm, rear—8 mm, floor—6 mm
Weight	8,900 kg (8.8 tons)
Dimensions:	*Length*—5.80 m (19 ft.)
	Height—2.10 m (6 ft. 11 in.)
	Width—2. 10 m (6 ft. 11 in.)
Engine	Maybach HL 42 TUKRM 6-cyl water-cooled; 100 HP
Speed	Road—52 km/h (32 mph)
Range	Road—320 km (199 miles)
	Cross-country—175 km (109 miles)
Production	Approx. 16,000 vehicles of all versions

Also used in action were a limited number of SdKfz 251 which mounted three 28 cm HE (high explosive) or 32 cm jellied-petrol rockets, with their launchers, on either side of the superstructure.

Panzer grenadiers dismounting from their SdKfz 250 during a reconnaissance mission.

An SdKfz 250/3 named 'Greif' (Griffin) being used by Rommel to observe a desert battle.

Light Armoured Personnel Carrier

The development history of the SdKfz 250, the German light armoured personnel carrier, was similar to that of the SdKfz 251. In 1933, the Army Ordnance Office asked Demag to develop a tractor capable of drawing a load of one ton. Two years later, a half-track prototype was being tested, and in 1939 full production of the *leichter Zugkraftwagen 1t SdKfz 10* was ordered. In that year too, following the acceptance of the SdKfz 251, it was realised that what was possible with the 3-ton chassis was also possible with the 1-ton. This proved to be of immense use to the Army, for it then required three special vehicles similar to, but smaller than, the SdKfz 251: one, to be designated SdKfz 252, for carrying munitions for infantry assault-guns; another, the SdKfz 253, to act as an observer's vehicle for the infantry assault-gun battalions; and the third, the SdKfz 250, for providing a reconnaissance vehicle carrying an infantry section. For all these vehicles, an armoured body on a modified 1-ton chassis was believed to be appropriate. Of the three, the SdKfz 250 proved to be the most successful, and, in 1941, production of the other two was ended in its favour.

The SdKfz 250 was designed to carry infantry of up to a section in strength (6 men including the driver) in a reconnaissance role. Its smaller capacity compared to the SdKfz 251 was necessary so that the reconnaissance battalion could be provided with a larger number of vehicles than would otherwise have been the case, thereby giving it greater flexibility in its role. The prototype, which, in layout and construction closely resembled the SdKfz 251, was completed in 1940, and, after extensive trials, mass-production was ordered. The official designation of the new vehicle was *leichter gepanzerter Mannschaftskraft-wagen,* but in 1942 it was retitled *leichter Schützenpanzerwagen.* In 1943, the SdKfz 250 was considerably redesigned along with the SdKfz 251, so as to facilitate assembly.

The SdKfz 250 carried 6 men, weighed from 5.38–5.6 tons, and had 12 official variants. They were as follows:

SdKfz 250/1	light armoured personnel carrier—one model carried a machine-gun in a heavy mounting, so that sustained supporting fire could be directed on distant targets.
SdKfz 250/2	field telephone cable layer.
SdKfz 250/3	radio command vehicle of which there were 4 types, with a crew of 4 and one machine-gun.
SdKfz 250/4	assault-gun observation vehicle to replace the SdKfz 253.
SdKfz 250/5 I and II	artillery observation vehicle.

SdKfz 250/6	ammunition carrier for assault-guns, to replace the SdKfz 252.
SdKfz 250/7	equipped with a medium 81 mm mortar.
SdKfz 250/8	equipped with a 7.5 cm KwK 37L/24.
SdKfz 250/9	equipped with a 2 cm KwK 38L/55 for recce duties.
SdKfz 250/10	equipped with a 3.7 cm Pak for platoon leaders.
SdKfz 250/11	equipped with a 2.8 cm sPz B41 tapered-bore anti-tank gun.
SdKfz 250/12	artillery survey vehicle.

There were also a number of unofficial versions of the SdKfz 250, some of which mounted a 2 cm Flak or KwK.

Light armoured personnel carrier SdKfz 250

Details (basic model)

Crew	6 men (driver and half-section of 5 panzer grenadiers)
Armament	1 x 7.92 mm MG 34 or 42, 1 sub-machine gun, 3-4 rifles)
Armour	Front—12 mm, side—7 mm, rear—7 mm, floor—6 mm
Weight	5,700 kg (5.6 tons)
Dimensions:	*Length*—4.56 m (14 ft. 11½ in.)
	Height—1.98 m (6 ft 6 in)
	Width—1.95 m (6 ft. 5 in)
Engine	Maybach HL 42 TRKM 6-cyl water-cooled; 100 HP
Speed	Road—65 km/h (40.4 mph)
Range	Road—350 km (217.5 miles)
	Cross-country—200 km (124 miles)
Production	Approx. 7,500 vehicles of all versions

Assault-guns

In 1936, as evidence of the fierce struggle between the infantry and the armour schools, the Army Ordnance Office ordered the development of an armoured infantry-support vehicle, mounting the 7.5 cm L/24 gun then being used on the PzKw IV tank. Krupp was given the responsibility of dealing with the gun and mounting, Daimler-Benz with the chassis and superstructure. The following year, five prototypes were built, based on the PzKw III *Ausf F* chassis, mounting a 7.5 cm howitzer in a low, fixed superstructure. The production machine was known as the *gepanzerte Selbstfahrlafette für Sturmgeschütz 7.5 cm Kanone Ausf.A, SdKfz (142 StuG III Ausf.A)* (armoured self-propelled mount for assault-gun 7.5 cm cannon). With low silhouette and fairly thick armour, the *StuG* III was relatively inexpensive to produce compared to a tank, and proved itself of value in the field during the invasion of the West in 1940, when four batteries were used. Capable of a

An assault gun detachment moving up to front in Italy in summer 1944.

An assault gun, armed with the short-barrelled 7.5 cm L/24 gun, carrying motorised infantrymen into battle.

An assault gun armed with the long 7.5 cm L/48 gun on PzKw IV chassis carrying a group of panzer grenadiers in Tunisia early in 1943.

Eastern Front, 1943. Panzer grenadiers ride through a field of corn atop an assault gun armed with a 10.5 cm howitzer. Note the close-fitting 'Saukopf' (Boars Head) type gun mantlet.

maximum speed of 25 mph on roads, the *StuG* III *Ausf.A* weighed 22 tons, had a maximum armour thickness of 50 mm and carried a crew of four.

Improvements upon the basic design were incorporated into *Ausf.B, C, D* and *E*. However, in 1941, with the shock of the superiority of the Soviet T-34 and KV-1 tanks, Hitler ordered that the *StuG* III be considerably up-gunned, and the *Ausf.F* was fitted with a long-barrelled 7.5 cm gun, the *StuK* 40 *(Sturmgeschütz-Kanone)*, and was given extra armour plates at the same time. With its high muzzle velocity, this gun was to prove an effective weapon, especially when combined with the low-silhouette of the *StuG* III. This vehicle appeared in early 1942.

However, because of the increasing use being made of the long 7.5 cm-armed *StuG* III as an anti-tank, rather than an infantry-support, weapon, (by the spring of 1944, *StuG* III's had destroyed 20,000 enemy tanks) it was thought necessary to again provide the infantry with a specially designed assault-gun. The first effort in this direction lay in the equipping some of the *Ausf.F's* with a modified 10.5 cm light field howitzer, designated *Sturmhaubitze 42* or *StuH* 42 (Assault Howitzer). This was but a temporary measure, and in early 1943 there appeared the final production model of the *StuG* III series, the *Ausf.G* with a 10.5 cm *StuH*.

The *StuG* III *Ausf.G* remained in production from early 1943 to the end of the war; as a result, there were introduced a number of variations with the passage of time, most noticeable of all being the introduction of the *Saukopf* (Boars Head) gun mantlet. *Zimmerit*—anti-magnetic cement was added to the superstructure to prevent the placing of magnetic mines, and side-plates were hung as protection against hollow-charge explosive rockets.

Prologue to Battle

The opening chapters of this book will already have shown in figures how few battalions were equipped with armoured carriers and thus proved how inaccurate was the belief that the grenadiers fought mounted all the time. This was Nazi propaganda at its best—*non e vero ma ben trovato*—and like successful propaganda the legend persists. The concept of the carrier-borne thrust into the enemy's defences may have been the ideal but reality was very different. Most battalions were equipped with unarmoured lorries and there was, therefore, a need for different tactics. Instead of driving into the heart of the enemy's positions and fighting him from the vehicles it was more usual for the grenadiers to be debussed at a· forming up, or less frequently a start line from whence they carried out conventional infantry assaults. But whether mounted in armour or carried in soft-skin vehicles or even clinging to the outside of panzers as they roared into battle, the panzer grenadiers were vital to the German conception of mobile, all-arms, strategic warfare as it should be fought in the fourth decade of the 20th century.

It must be understood that in isolation and by themselves panzer grenadiers could win no wars and, indeed, only in conjunction with tanks did they have any offensive, strategic potential. This is not to say that they had only tactical value for they often proved to be of strategic worth in certain defensive battle situations.

This part of the book cannot record, therefore, vast war-winning offensives and all-out assaults leading to military successes, but it does record the service of the 'hand maids' of the panzer divisions, those men who went into the attack generally unprotected by armour plate.

The accounts which are given here show the panzer grenadiers in both attack and defence although it is true to say that no battle is wholly either offensive or defensive. For in every defensive action there are moments when attack is demanded just as in every offensive posture there comes the time when the forward momentum is halted, momentarily, under an enemy counter thrust. Thus in every one of these accounts the panzer grenadier can be seen as the all-round specialist soldier.

The first account describes the action of *Das Reich* Panzer Grenadier Division in 'Operation Typhoon', the thrust for Moscow in the autumn of 1941. Here the intention is to show a panzer grenadier division in an

Camouflaged SdKfz 251's during the German advance in the South Ukraine.

offensive and strategic situation. Then follows the description of the defensive role played by the Grenadier regiments of the 'Hitler Youth' Division in Normandy during the early summer of 1944. In this account the regiments' action are seen to have strategic implications. In the third account part of a grenadier battalion of the Waffen-SS in a tactical situation can be seen to have achieved a strategic victory by a combination of luck, aggression and determination. The fourth and final account is the action by the *Brandenburg* Division of the *Grossdeutschland* Corps whose brilliant defence and defensive tactics achieved a major tactical success in the last weeks of the Second World War.

That three of the four accounts recorded here refer to Waffen-SS troops is coincidental and not deliberate for, whether by accident or design, those units seem to have been in the most exciting battles at the crucial times. Let their actions also speak for the great mass of panzer grenadiers who fought the less glamorous, 'run of the mill' battles and who are, here, unrecorded.

2nd Waffen-SS Division 'Das Reich' in Advance on Moscow, October 1941

By the middle of September 1941, the German armies which had invaded the Soviet Union during June of that year had captured vast areas of territory and, in fierce fighting, had won victories in which more than a million Red Army soldiers had been taken prisoner. Encouraged by the successes of the late summer and early autumn, the German Army Groups North, Centre and South prepared to resume the advance towards their respective principal objectives; Leningrad, Moscow and the Ukraine.

This account deals specifically with the two Grenadier regiments *Der Führer* and *Deutschland,* which together made up the lorried infantry component of the Waffen-SS Division *Das Reich,* and records the battles which they fought in the opening stages of 'Operation Typhoon', Army Group Centre's offensive in the late autumn of 1941.

The two SS regiments had fought within the establishment of several units in the opening campaigns of the Second World War and as *Das Reich* Division had taken an active part in the attack on the Soviet Union. After a period of rest, during which their terrible losses had been made good, they were posted to XL Corps, part of Panzer Group 4, where together with 10th Panzer Division, also in XL Corps, they formed the spearhead of the Panzer Group's attack up the Roslavl—Moscow road. By cutting this highway the north/south flow of Red Army troops would be halted and then *Das Reich* Division was to advance up the road to the junction of the main Smolensk—Moscow highway. The SS Division would then force the attack eastwards along the road pressing the advance towards the Soviet capital. It is this fighting which is described here.

Bitter experience in the summer campaign of the imprisoning mud into which the Russian soil and roads were transmuted by only moderate rainfall, had demonstrated to the Germans how vital was the need to seize the few metalled all-weather highways which led towards the interior of the Soviet homeland. The fighting which is described here was of such a nature that the greatest burden fell upon the grenadiers. One of the principal advantages of such an arm of service, according to German Field Regulations, was that grenadiers were not defeated by conditions of climate or terrain. But Russian mud which had stopped completely all German wheeled traffic and had inhibited severely the movement of even tanks and tracked vehicles nearly halted

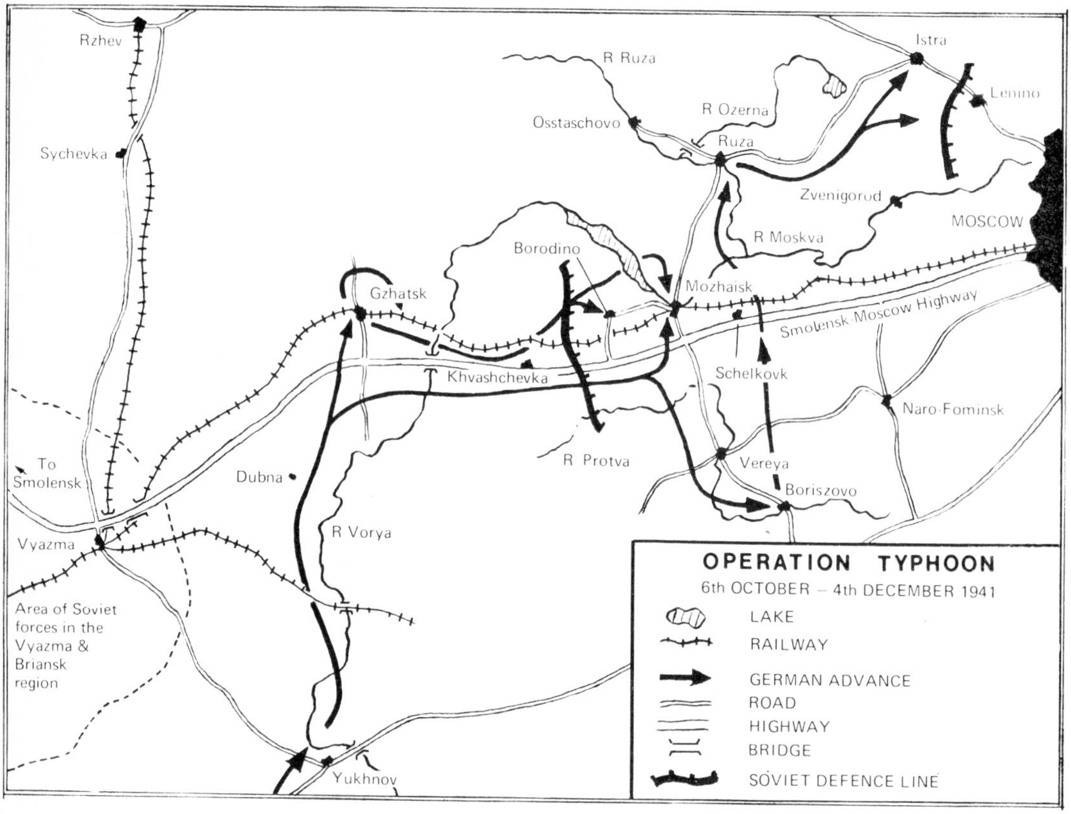

Rzhev
Sychevka
To Smolensk
Vyazma
Area of Soviet forces in the Vyazma & Briansk region
Dubna
R Vorya
Yukhnov
Gzhatsk
Khvashchevka
Borodino
R Protva
R Ruza
Osstaschovo
R Ozerna
Ruza
Istra
Lenino
Zvenigorod
MOSCOW
R Moskva
Mozhaisk
Smolensk-Moscow Highway
Schelkovk
Naro-Fominsk
Vereya
Boriszovo
OPERATION TYPHOON
6th OCTOBER – 4th DECEMBER 1941
LAKE
RAILWAY
GERMAN ADVANCE
ROAD
HIGHWAY
BRIDGE
SOVIET DEFENCE LINE

the grenadiers as well. It had an exhausting demoralising effect upon them for they often had to attack through mud which was usually so thick and deep that their assaults were at slow motion pace. The men helped one another to extricate themselves from the clinging mud weighing down their boots and clothes as they struggled forward. To the misery of fighting through such conditions and of sleeping out, night after night, in the open country there was added the early winter cold; not sufficient to freeze the ground and thus harden it for tank operations, but enough to paralyse the senses of the soldiers standing in their slit trenches.

But that is to anticipate events; it was bright weather for the opening of 'Operation Typhoon', the advance towards Moscow. It was obvious to OKW, the German High Command, that an assault upon the Soviet capital would be met with the most determined, indeed ruthless resistance, and it was known that the city was surrounded by strong defensive positions. Nevertheless, it was hoped that the momentum of the assault would carry it through this resistance and across those defences so that Moscow, the Army Group objective would be captured before the onset of winter.

The Soviet government, deeply conscious of the grave situation, not only raised three armies from the citizens of Moscow and sent these up the line, but when Smolensk fell had enlisted 100,000 civilians to dig trench systems in the Vyasma and Mozhaisk regions. That these were

Eastern Front, 1943. Waffen-SS panzer grenadiers hurry past a destroyed Soviet T-34/76C tank.

completed within a week shows how aware was the Soviet High Command to the strategic importance of those areas, and in them STAVKA, the Soviet General Headquarters, massed no fewer than 40% of all its infantry and artillery as well as 35% of all available armour. It was confidently believed that with this mass of men and protected by the defences the German offensive might be halted.

The OKW plan was for armoured thrusts to bypass and to encircle the Soviet troops in the Vyasma and Briansk areas, whereupon, with those forces neutralised, the German infantry would make a frontal assault upon Moscow while the panzers flung a pair of pincer arms to the north and south of the city.

'Operation Typhoon', Army Group Centre's offensive opened in brilliant autumn weather and the fast advances made during the first two days of operations encouraged the hope that the Red Army would be met and destroyed once and for all, and this time before the gates of Moscow itself. By 4 October three Soviet armies, 30th, 19th and 43rd had been forced to withdraw to avoid encirclement, the troops in front of Vyasma had been taken back to form a shorter line and German pressure during 6 October had forced STAVKA to authorise further retreats. The Soviet front was beginning to fragment, the 31st Red Army was isolated and it seemed as if nothing could halt the German panzer thrusts.

Panzer grenadiers attacking a enemy position. Fitted with a 50-round drum magazine the MG 34 machine gun could be fired by one man on the move.

The SS Division *Das Reich* came into the line on 6 October and was given the task of advancing to seize the area between Gzhatsk and Vyasma, to cut the Smolensk—Moscow highway and to hold its ground against the attempts of the Red Army to break into or out of the ring at Vyasma within which its units were encircled.

The divisional reconnaissance battalion and the motorcycle battalion led the race northwards, leaving behind them the grenadiers of *Deutschland* regiment marching into battle. Shortly after the advance began several groups of Soviet motorised troops which had broken through the German ring and which were trying to regain touch with their main forces, struck across the grenadiers' front and after a short fierce fire fight were driven back. This was only the first of the many minor battles that *Deutschland* had to fight that day for the deeper the SS advance drove into the Russian rear areas the greater grew the intensity of the Soviet opposition. Red assault aircraft swept low over the SS columns bombing and strafing, sometimes slowing but never halting the onrushing grenadiers. At a tactically important hill on the line of advance the tenacious Russian defence halted the reconnaissance battalion's forward movement, and not until a grenadier battalion was put in to collaborate with the recce unit did the hill fall to the Germans. At last light the motor cycle battalion took over as advance guard and in a set piece night attack 3rd Grenadier battalion, together with the point unit, seized the road and rail bridges at Yegorye Kuleshi and set up bridgeheads on either side of the highway.

The crossroads town of Gzhatsk was an important one, vital indeed

Waffen-SS riflemen with a captured Soviet soldier during the advance into the Ukraine in early autumn 1941.

to both armies, for whoever held it could obstruct the free flowing movements of the other side and the battles of the next few days were fought around or against that town. At 08.00 hrs on 7 October the *Deutschland* regiment moved forward to cut the railway line to Gzhatsk and the east-west highway at Velichovo. The mobile elements, the motorcycle and the recce battalions, swung out to guard the division's right flank while the grenadier battalions opened the assault towards the initial objectives of Shavisky and Shatyescha bridges, supported by an artillery group of flak, anti-tank and SP guns.

Once again the Soviet forward line withdrew under SS pressure and drew back to a main area of resistance which was so strongly held that it could only be fought down by assault guns firing at point blank range. But by late morning a ridge to the northwest of Sharaponova was taken by 2nd Grenadier battalion who then pushed the advance so quickly forward that by tea time the village of Micheyeva had been taken. Its fall broke the Red resistance on that sector and battalion thrust into Slovoda Potovskaya, but even there the advance was still not allowed to halt for it was realised that any lessening of pressure would allow the Soviets to reform and renew their determined resistance. The 2nd battalion which had carried its share of the burden during that day halted while 1st Grenadier battalion, mounted in armoured personnel carriers, passed through and prepared to take up the pursuit. But the vehicles had not driven far when the appalling state of the roads halted them and the grenadiers were debussed and put into the attack on foot. Kámyonka, the day's objective fell to them at 23.00 hrs.

In obedience to Corps order to drive forward the advance and to capture Gzhatsk, Division regrouped and flung *Deutschland* into a mounted, three battalion advance. One battalion went forward, linked up with the recce battalion, which was lying in front of Mashina, and together they smashed their way towards the village of Pokrov. The remaining two battalions of the regiment were held ready to exploit any breakthrough to Gzhatsk. The importance of the town was not lost to the Soviets, who began the 8 October not by standing on the defensive but by flinging an attack in regimental strength against the reconnaissance battalion. Under the weight and fury of this assault the German drive faltered until the grenadiers swung out a Company to attack from the right flank while the main of the battalion drove in from the left. In another sector a grenadier battalion striking towards the ridge at Petyayka was pinned down by fanatical Soviet resistance and only the close support of heavy artillery was able to crush the enemy so that the SS men could move forward once again. It was clear that the battle for Gzhatsk would be a bitter and protracted affair.

At other parts of the line along which Army Group Centre was attacking German outflanking moves had forced the withdrawal of one group of four Red armies and a general move back to the Mozhaisk defence line had begun. It was to that sector that all available reserves of the Soviet forces had been concentrated and where a new Army, the 5th had been formed.

A group of PzKw II tanks temporarily held up by Soviet defences in summer 1941.

Slowly the skill and determination of the SS panzer grenadiers began to prevail and as the battalions of *Deutschland*, crushing all resistance, began to move forward along the entire regimental line, the Reds before them conformed and took part in the general withdrawal. The regimental objective—Pokrov—fell but the grenadiers were embussed without delay and assigned a new target—Nikolskoya. STAVKA massed troops to delay the SS thrust and the advance by 2nd battalion was slowed down until SP guns were brought up to smash the Red defenders. In reply the Soviets brought up their artillery to close range in an effort to hold the storming drive by the SS, but the SPs beat down the Soviet guns and destroyed the batteries as they tried to withdraw across the open fields. The Luftwaffe too, collaborated with the ground troops in the destruction of the Soviet forces by machine-gunning the Russian soldiers and defences. By mid-afternoon Nikols-koya had also been captured but still no halt was allowed and in blinding flurries of the first snowstorms the grenadiers of 1st battalion were embussed and sent forward, closely followed by the men of 3rd battalion. By 20.00 hrs the SS had cut the Moscow highway and at last the widely spread-out battalions of *Deutschland* regiment were allowed to halt, but not to rest, for they maintained patrols throughout the night.

Corps issued orders that on 9 October *Das Reich* Division was to link up with 10th Panzer Division and that together they were to carry the advance eastwards. *Deutschland* mounted a two battalion attack at dawn

Above left: *Waffen-SS infantrymen of the motorised regiment 'Germania' in France, 1940. Note that all SS collar patches have been removed.*

Above: *A group of exhausted Waffen-SS infantrymen after battle.*

A mortar section crossing a stream aboard an assault boat. Note the exposed position of the rear outboard engine operator.

and the grenadiers moved off through the blinding blizzard, still dressed in their European pattern overcoats which did not keep out the bitter cold of the Russian winter. For the assault the battalions had been given extra artillery support behind whose deluge of shells a battle group entered the southern part of the town, moving forward all the time despite the low-flying Soviet assault aircraft which strafed and bombed even individual groups of soldiers. A quick thrust through the woods outside the town carried out by 1st battalion, wrested a defensive position from the Soviets and their immediate response was to counter attack. Three assaults in quick succession were hurled against the grenadiers' left wing slowing down the advance, but the right flank SS attack had an easier passage and not only destroyed a great number of the enemy but overran field defences outside the town. Onward pushed a second battalion across a railway enbankment and finally into Gzhatsk itself. Then their first footholds were extended until the eastern and northern parts of the town had been occupied. SS artillery, up with the forward Companies, fired upon Red columns fleeing from the town's northern exists and destroyed them.

The 3rd battalion assault had also made such good progress and by midday the rest of the town had been captured and patrols had combed the area outside for Red stragglers. These were added to the 500 prisoners which the regiment had taken during the battle for Gzhatsk, and as evidence of the collapse of Soviet resistance in that sector one of the combing patrols reported that the Russians were moving back so quickly that they had not halted at the next village but had continued their retreat past that place.

On 9 October, *Deutschland's* sister regiment in *Das Reich* Division, *Der Führer*, came into the line and was put in on the right wing. Once again the orders were to renew the advance up the Moscow highway and *Der Führer* regiment decided on a two battalion assault at dawn. The advance began and met large numbers of disorganised Russian soldiers moving through the area and who were attempting to break through eastwards across the regiment's line of advance. This mob of men was quickly driven back. STAVKA gave to the mass of the Red Army trapped in the Vyasma and the Briansk pockets the task of gaining time for the Mozhaisk line to be manned, but the Soviet attempts to hold firm positions in front of the town were made more difficult, and the situation became very fluid as Corps and Armies withdrew from their positions in order not to be outflanked and surrounded.

Not at every point was resistance weak, and along the line of advance of *Der Führer* regiment the Russian defence was tenacious. In one village against which 2nd battalion had gone out in a wide flanking movement, heavy Russian fire forced the grenadiers to ground in the open, snow covered fields. They lay there, conspicuous in their dark overcoats and began to suffer heavy losses. To lay there was to be killed; to advance was less dangerous, and the officers by personal examples of bravery and contempt of death brought the men to their feet and they stormed into the village. The regiment consolidated in the afternoon upon its objective, taking up defensive positions facing north-east against the Red infantry and tank attacks coming out of Slovoda. The assaulting waves, striking forward against the SS hedgehog positions, were driven off with heavy loss to the attackers.

A 3.7 cm Pak 36 anti-tank gun mounted on an SdKfz 250/10. Note the cut-down armour protection for the crew compared to the standard shield of this gun.

During the day the divisional motorcycle battalion linked with 10th Panzer Division and both units then co-operated in destroying Soviet traffic fleeing eastwards up the road. Two lorries at the head of one column and crammed with Red Army men were bombarded and caught fire. The Red infantry streamed across the fields. The burning vehicles obstructed the advance of the column and when the last lorry was also set alight, neither could the column retreat. The SS machine gunners and panzer men opened up on the lines of halted trucks killing and wounding many of the occupants. The survivors surrendered. The motorcyclists remounted their machines and drove through the Russian areas overrunning small and scattered groups of the enemy. Feeling the SS so close behind them many broke easily but one group was made up of men of sterner stuff, officer cadets who fought bitterly. As their casualities mounted this group split up into small detachments and then into individual soldiers until, eventually, only one man was left. He died defiantly. This fanatical resistance had allowed the Soviet resistance to coalesce, and late in the afternoon the SS thrust met determined opposition which had not been broken by last light and fighting continued throughout the night.

Despite the STAVKA order to go over to the defensive many Red commanders at local level mounted attacks one of which, just after midnight, produced a crisis for the SS south of the road. A grenadier company was attacked by a combined infantry and armour force and bitter fighting lasted until the Red tanks had been destroyed in close combat. Thwarted at that point, other Soviet thrusts came in all through the remainder of the night against the remaining companies and dawn light exposed yet another infantry assault advancing across the snow covered ground towards the village. This attack, too, was broken by mortar fire and flung back by the SS grenadiers. But still the local Red commander put in men and tanks so that fighting continued around that village until 11 October.

As a result of a change in the Red leadership, General Zhukov who was now in overall command on that Front quickly reshuffled his Armies. The 16th Army took over along the Volokolamzk sector, the 5th held the Mozhaisk region, 43rd the Maloyaroslavets and 49th—the Kaluga sector. Behind these and further to strengthen the defences around Moscow another trench line, parallel to that in the Mozhaisk sector, was contructed.

Division then received intelligence of a Red build up east of Gzhatsk and to throw this off balance a spoiling attack was launched by *Der Führer* regiment at 08.00 hrs. In a bitterly fought engagement the SS regiment captured the heights west of Slovoda and went on to crush the Soviet 18th Armoured Brigade by SP artillery fire. By nightfall the line Slovoda—Gzhatsk had been reached, but the heavy fighting had cost *Der Führer* regiment dear. Losses to the Division in an offensive which had barely run a week exceeded 500 men killed, wounded and missing.

A patrol report that the Soviets were either preparing defensive positions or were withdrawing brought the order that Division was to exploit this weakness by a pursuit of the enemy leading to the capture of Mozhaisk. The SS advance would be unsupported, but once the

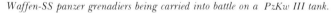

Waffen-SS panzer grenadiers being carried into battle on a PzKw III tank.

Riflemen accompanying an assault-gun into a Russian village in autumn 1941.

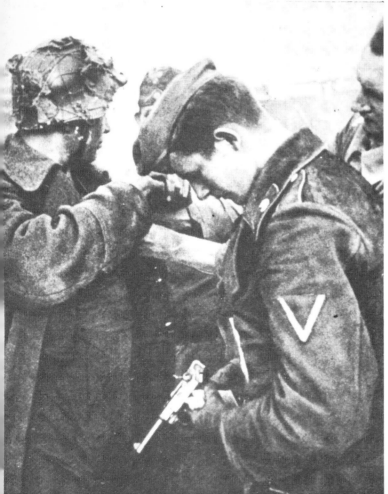

Riflemen and tank crews after a battle.

encirclement operation around Vyansk had been completed a panzer regiment from 10th Panzer Division would move up in support and other units as they became free. But initially the SS Division would be facing the whole of 5th Red Army.

At 10.00 hrs on 11 October, two battle groups moved over the start line. On the left grenadier regiment *Deutschland,* with strong artillery and assault engineer support, had the task of thrusting from Gzhatsk to Mozhaisk and of attracting Soviet attention away from the main blow which would be carried out by *Der Führer* regiment. The composition of *Der Führer* battle group was the same as that of *Deutschland,* except for an 8.8 cm Flak gun which accompanied the artillery units. The Soviet commander was not long deceived as to which was the main effort and although, initially, the attack by *Der Führer* flowed forward, determined resistance backed by an armoured train soon began to slow it down. Russian tenacity together with the appalling conditions in the open land halted the forward drive of *Der Führer's* 1st battalion as it moved along the side of the road, and the other two battalions were involved in close combat for a vast and heavily wooded area. To support the grenadiers in their battle Corps at last put in the panzer regiment, allotting a battalion to each of the SS regiments.

The panzer battalion supporting *Der Führer* swung north of the road and attacked the woods with all guns blazing. Out of the dark forest roared a wave of Soviet T-34's and into them smashed a hail of armour-piercing shells from the guns of the panzers and the SPs. Within 10 minutes the Soviets had lost one third of their armoured strength, and under the punishing fire the remaining vehicles withdrew into the shelter of the trees. The failure of their armour to drive back the panzers brought about a collapse of Russian resistance in that sector and taking advantage of this temporary weakness the *Der Führer* grenadiers, in a sudden thrust, smashed into and through the Russian field fortifications.

On the sector held by *Deutschland* regiment the grenadiers went in with a swing overrunning enemy trench systems and pressing forward, until the momentum of the attack was slowed by the appearance on the field of some super-heavy Russian tanks which rolled out of cover and bombarded the German line. From the SS positions rose the violet coloured flares 'We are under tank attack' and at once the artillery moved forward. Their guns had no effect upon the thick armour plate of the enourmous vehicles and only the heavy artillery, firing special armour-piercing shells, was able to break up and to drive back the Red tank attack. By 11.00 hrs 1st and 3rd battalions of *Deutschland* had reached the first objectives and had pushed on to the village of Paleninova. Without pause the assault flowed towards the heights east of Kuryanova and was about to scale these when another Soviet tank thrust came in against it. But the grenadiers would not be held and repelled the enemy armour. Then from the forests poured wave after wave of T-34's threatening to halt the advance, but the SS, using every fold in the flat plain across which they were attacking, gained the cover of the trees and struck at the Soviet tanks in single close combat destroying them with explosive charges. More T-34's rolled into the woods to expel the grenadiers but the SS artillery, firing over open sights, destroyed some Soviet tanks at ranges no greater than 300 metres and forced the others to draw back. At night the *Deutschland* soldiers and the artillerymen went into all round defence, ready to resume the drive on the following morning.

During the morning of 12 October *Der Führer* troops attacked with panzer support and by midday had broken into and through a series of trench systems and permanent defensive positions which the Soviets had erected. One of the SS companies supported by dive bombing Ju 87's pursued a group of Russian troops up the motorway and destroyed tanks, anti-aircraft and anti-tank guns.

A handful of panzers led 1st and 3rd battalions of *Deutschland* regiment across the regimental start line at dawn while 2nd battalion, carried on the remainder of the vehicles, was held as a mobile reserve ready to exploit any breakthrough. Red armour and infantry counter-attacks came in along the whole of the line but were beaten off and the advance continued, but at a very slow pace for the ground over which the regiment attacked was mud which bogged down the tanks. For the grenadiers each footstep was a battle against the weight of the mud clinging to the boots and a struggle to extricate a leg to make another step. Despite the bitter cold the grenadiers sweated in the advance and a hundred metres was an exhausting physical effort. Nevertheless, the pace of the assault was maintained and by 07.30 hrs the village of Shulevo had been reached.

Riflemen accompanying a PzKw II on a raid behind the main combat line in 1941 during which they blew up a Soviet armoured train.

The strain of battle shows on the faces of these panzer grenadiers during the bitter fighting in the Soviet Union in 1941.

The rearward movement by the Soviet field units was repeated in the major formations and by mid-October the whole of the right wing of the Fronts facing the Germans was in full retreat. The 29th Army faced encirclement but was withdrawn in time. Seven infantry Divisions taken from the right wing were put into the defence of the Mozhaisk sector and, southeast of Rhzev, Army Group Centre had reached the southern bank of the Volga. By 14 October Kalinin to the north of Moscow had fallen and the Front flank was threatened, but a speedy withdrawal to a shorter line released troops to be sent to bolster the Mozhaisk sector. And just in time, for that area was then struck by a heavy infantry and panzer attack. Among the forces defending the Mozhaisk sector was Polushkin's 321st Infantry Division and three armoured brigades, and it was upon them that the storming SS Division made its assaults.

Along the regimental front of *Deutschland* the advance continued until a bridgehead across the Konollyovka river had been established. Against this rapid drive the Russians flung one counter-attack after another seeking with armour to halt the SS infantry. Against these Soviet armoured attacks the German panzers battled and won and although the pace of the advance was slow it was constant and continued until Drovino, the day's objective, had been reached. The SS commander was convinced that his grenadiers could still gain ground and advanced upon Papovka, which was captured at 15.00 hrs and where a link up was effected with the men of *Der Führer* regiment. *Deutschland* renewed the attack at 06.30 hrs on 13 October with 3rd battalion mounted on tanks but with the infantry of the other two battalions going in on foot for the thick mud had halted all wheeled traffic. At about 09.30 hrs Kolozhkoya was reached and defensive positions dug while No. 9 Company went out to reconnoitre for

Riflemen and tanks on the Eastern Front in 1941. The tanks are PzKw III's, armed with 3.7 cm guns.

crossing points across the stream in the area of Rogachevo. This daring group penetrated the Soviet defensive positions and thus it was a small SS patrol which was the first German unit to test the defences of the Moscow defensive line. With panzer support the Company breached part of the outer defences and the regimental commander then decided to fling his unit through the breach with all three battalions up, even though he was now unsupported by the tanks which had gone back under command of 10th Panzer Division. Corps released to Division the 54th *Nebelwerfer* (rocket launcher) regiment and batteries of 8.8 cm Flak guns were brought forward to beat back any Red tank thrusts. Under a brief but heavy bombardment 1st battalion of *Deutschland* broke into the positions, overran a surprised enemy and made such good progress that Regiment could report to Division by 16.00 hrs that it had penetrated to a depth of 3 kms and had reached Yelnya. During the evening and night the penetrations were broadened and deepened.

The 3rd battalion *Der Führer* mounted on panzers carried that regiment's advance during 13 October farther up the highway, and a sudden frost which had hardened the ground allowed the grenadiers to move forward in wheeled transport. By afternoon reconnaissance had shown that the Soviet defensive positions were made up of five strong lines extending to a depth of 2 kms and supported by dug-in tank turrets, flame throwers and backed by artillery. It would be a formidable undertaking and because of the ground conditions it would have to be a wholly grenadier operation.

The panzer spearhead advanced as far as it could, then took up position while two grenadier battalions moved forward to test the extent and the strength of the Russian defences. The hour and place of the original attack, which had been timed to begin at dawn on 14 October, were advanced because of the success of *Deutschland* regiment's thrust and the main effort by *Der Führer* was made on its 3rd battalion's sector. The grenadiers moved through the Soviet defences in pouring rain and sleet showers, fighting down the resistance put up by the Russian soldiers. The men of 32nd Siberian Rifle Division, reinforced by two armoured brigades, battled with an unusual ferocity against the SS. The fighting was almost exclusively hand to hand, with the grenadiers battling their way from one strong point to another beating down the giant Siberians with entrenching tools and clubs, until they had penetrated the whole defence system on a narrow frontage. Against fanatical resistance 1st battalion reached an area north west of Yelnya and there joined hands with *Deutschland* at 20.15 hrs. Division was ordered to clear the area between Karshen and Borodino, then to go on to take Mozhaisk and to carry the assault on to Russa. This would be no easy task, yet it was expected of men who had been fighting a bitter battle without respite, with no changes of clothes, warm accommodation or even hot food, for the field kitchens could not be brought forward through the mud.

The fighting lasted all night, and in close quarter battles the two Grenadier regiments of *Das Reich* Division increased the depth of their penetrations. On 14 October the 2nd battalion *Der Führer* was ordered to exploit the gap southwards so that the waiting armour of 10th Panzer Division could pass through, while *Deutschland* put up all three battalions to clear the wooded area to the east of Yelnya. These battalions were on their objective by 11.15 hrs and the Soviets were in full flight eastwards. Although *Der Führer* had widened the breach the ground conditions did not allow the armour to be put in and then the SS infantry fighting against the heavily reinforced Soviets realised that for all their struggles they had only pierced the outer defences of the Moscow line. Neverthless the grenadiers were given the task of capturing Artemki without panzer support, but this attack proved abortive. Red assaults in battalion strength drove back the *Der Führer* battalions and elements from *Deutschland* had to be brought in to restore the situation.

The force of Soviet counter-attacks diminished and the SS resumed their advance. Two of *Der Führer* battalions moved upon Borodino while the third, still struggling in the Moscow defence position, was widening the breach which it had created in expectation of the arrival of 10th Panzer Division. The panzer regiment of that formation had been battling its way through towards Borodino which it then captured with the support of the SS battalions. The fighting for the high ground at that place was hard; very hard. But the *elan* of the grenadiers at last fought down the Siberian defenders and with the fall of Borodino the key to the first defensive position on the road to Moscow had been taken.

Rain and snow had now made even the road as impassable to wheeled traffic as the ground had long since been and the strain became more difficult. Sheer exhaustion was slowing the pace of the advance, and despite the losses which both grenadier regiments had suffered the number of replacements received had been insufficient to keep the companies up to strength.

For the 16 October the divisional tasks were to enlarge the area of penetration both to the north and south. The attacks went in through blizzards so dense that the grenadiers frequently lost sight of each other and all of them had the feeling that they were advancing alone against the Russian positions. In this belief they were not altogether wrong for so great had been their losses that company strengths were down to only 35 men, the strength of a weak platoon. The *Deutschland* regiment continued the battle for Borodino and was held at the railway station until the divisional motorcycle battalion was put in and brought the attack forward.

Mozhaisk was still the objective, and while 10th Panzer Division battled towards the town the SS Division was set the task of capturing the crossroads 6 km to the southwest. At a time when the grenadiers were battling for every yard of ground against an impacable enemy an Intelligence report claimed that the encirclement battles had so destroyed the Russian forces that east of Gzhatsk the Red Army Command had been unable to put organised units into the field. Whether Corps believed this the grenadiers fighting often hand to hand against a fanatical, well equipped enemy strongly supported by massed artillery and better armour, knew how inaccurate such a statement was, just as they knew that the Soviets were reinforcing their troops on the Artemki sector with first-class units and with heavy concentrations of armoured fighting vehicles.

Once again on 17 October, dawn saw the SS grenadiers preparing to resume the attack eastwards. *Deutschland* was to open the assault while *Der Führer*, with heavy artillery support and together with the motor-cycle battalion was to be held back until *Deutschland's* attack succeeded. Then *Der Führer* regiment would exploit the break through. *Deutschland* moved off at 08.00 hrs and swung out so as to take Artemki from the north, but within an hour the first Russian counter-attacks had halted the grenadier advance. Two battalions were swung into a flanking assault against the woods west of Artemki and fighting hard against Red snipers, tanks and through a strong defensive barrage they had crossed an anti-tank ditch, passed through the forests and reached the northwestern outskirts of the town. Under the cover of a sudden and heavy Stuka bombardment the battalions stormed into Artemki capturing it and consolidating it by 20.00 hrs. This cornerstone of the Moscow Defence Line and its defenders had prevented the advance of the SS regiments. Now it had fallen and with it collapsed the Russian determination on that sector. Sivkova fell to the storming assault of *Der*

Panzer grenadiers supported by an assault gun during a local counter-attack.

Waffen-SS panzer grenadier engineers in the Soviet Union during the winter of 1943. The SdKfz 251's carry bridging equipment on their sides.

Führer regiment but Russian heavy artillery firing 'rolling barrages' to cover the withdrawal of the Red infantry, slowed the pace of the advance.

As a pre-condition for the forthcoming grand assault upon Moscow Corps was ordered to capture Vereya and Mozhaisk and to go on to seize strong bridgeheads across the Moskva river. *Das Reich* was ordered to gain the cross roads on the Axyenyevo—Mozhaisk highway from which the assault upon the town would be made, and Division gave this task to *Der Führer* regiment.

The 18 October dawned bright and cold and the cloudless sky allowed Stuka bombers to give close and effective support sweeping down, attacking and destroying Red tanks and artillery in the crossroads area. As soon as the Ju 87's flew away from out of the woods Russian tank waves flowed down upon the advancing SS column, firing at long range on the motorcycle advanced guard and the grenadiers of *Der Führer* regiment. SP's from the SS Division engaged the Red armour and soon fires from burning T-34's and ammunition littered the open countryside. The Soviet tanks withdrew. By afternoon the SS advance had pushed eastward to a depth of 6 kms against determined resistance. In one sector the Red troops of the rearguard fought to the death to delay the German advance while their comrades tried to escape in vehicles, but the mobile SS artillery at point blank range took the fleeing columns under a heavy and accurate fire. The Soviet losses were enormous.

Slowly the German grenadiers struggled to attain their objective and the nearer they approached the cross roads the more the fighting grew in intensity. Battling bitterly against the determined resistance of the Red troops the SS finally tore the cross roads from their enemy's grasp.

The attack by *Deutschland* regiment on 18 October moved off along the highway but had not made much ground when Russian tanks drove out of the woods and opened fire. The SS self-propelled artillery swung towards the armoured wedge and drove it back into the forests. The immediate defeat of their armour broke the resistance of the Red troops in the area and the pace of the grenadier advance quickened, overrunning Soviet vehicle columns and penetrating into the rear areas. As the tempo of the chase quickened the SS troops battled their way forward with more *elan*, and in the late morning Division ordered the two leading battalions to swing north-eastwards to capture Sobolki while 3rd battalion went on to seize the village of Novosuryino. From that point the attack upon Mozhaisk began, and *Deutschland* opened the assault from the south while 10th Panzer Division drove into the town from the north. At 15.00 hrs two battalions thrust into the outskirts of the town while the third went out to capture the eastern heights. The battle along the road into the town had been fought tank against tank and SPs had been brought forward with the leading infantry companies to crush the Red resistance. In the narrow and blazing streets of Mozhaisk T-34's attacked the assaulting SS troops but were engaged in close combat with explosive charges and destroyed. The determined SS assault had split the Red forces in and around Mozhaisk and then had gone on to destroy the retreating Red remnants.

Waffen-SS panzer grenadiers in action in the bitter cold of the Russian winter.

SS patrols linked up with the men of 10th Panzer Division striking down from the north, and despite their exhaustion the grenadiers were ordered to clear more of the highway as far as Mikhailovskaya. The attack did not go in for the Red Command, desperate at the loss of Mozhaisk, the gateway to Moscow, flung in a succession of counter-attacks to regain the town. Tank assaults followed infantry attacks, the brown waves coming in across the snowy fields, mass upon mass of men thrown in to recapture the town regardless of loss. Some groups of Red infantry and tanks actually penetrated into the streets of Mozhaisk, driving back the men from 10th Panzer Division's lorried infantry.

During the 19 October the SS motor cycle battalion was put in to attack the cross roads east of Mozhaisk and to capture the town of Yasenov. The fighting was carried through thick forests with dense, matted undergrowth in which often lurked Red anti-tank guns and armour. The Russian defence was bitter and protracted. During the night of 19/20 October *Deutschland* was ordered to send a battalion through the woods to support the attack by *Der Führer*, while another battalion was to hedgehog round the cross roads once these had been seized. After regrouping the attack was to be pressed along the highway to Mikhailovskaya.

The fighting was hard and confused along the whole divisional front and an advance by 1st battalion to capture a tactically important point was held by Red artillery fire, while 3rd battalion could not press any farther forward than the southern end of the village of Yamskaya. Shortly after 10.00 hrs the motorcycle battalion found a weak spot, thrust through this and reached a point to the west of the crossroads. A grenadier battalion was immediately swung into an attack to exploit this situation advancing together with the motorcyclists. As the two battalion assault moved off Soviet armour and infantry smashed forward in a counter-attack against the grenadier battalion's flank. Halting to steady itself the SS battalion struck back at the advancing Soviet armour causing it severe losses and, swinging back immediately into the pace of the assault, had captured the crossroads by midday and there linked up with *Der Führer* regiment. The exhausted battalions were allowed to halt and not before time, for they had been in action without rest since 6 October. But however weak the SS regiments were they could not be spared from the line.

For 21 October the Division was ordered to continue the advance along the main road and to clear the ground south of the highway. At 07.15 hrs *Deutschland* moved off through a heavy bombardment which fell upon the concentration area, and pushed in Osyakovo without opposition. On the far side of the village bitter fighting broke out. As the first lines of grenadiers emerged from the low wooden houses they were taken in flank by battalions of Mongolian infantry from 82nd Division, supported by tanks and artillery. The forward movement of the SS regiment was halted and the companies formed front to take on the waves of Red infantry and armour which stormed towards them. The close supporting SS artillery fired over open sights into the Red infantry ranks and the concentrated groups of Soviet tanks. For over an hour and a half the attacks came in succession, and only when the Russian tide had ebbed back into the forests from which it had

Panzer grenadiers mount assault guns in preparation for an attack in winter fog.

A group of Waffen-SS riflemen being awarded the Iron Cross 2nd class.

emerged were the grenadiers conscious of the intense cold for the thermometer had dropped to 15 degrees below freezing. The SS battalion quickly regouped and drove forward across a battlefield which showed plainly that the battle had often been fought in hand to hand combats. Mikhailovskaya fell, then Grachevo, and the momentum of attack reached Pushkino. The Red defence was in confusion and the SS exploiting this pushed forward their SPs to shell the enemy columns retreating eastwards. Pushkino fell at 16.20 hrs and again there came the exhilaration of the chase as the tank-mounted grenadiers pursued the Soviet troops, overrunning a Red artillery column and its guns.

Der Führer regiment struck towards Borisovo, a town on a long ridge, in support of an assault by an infantry division. This attack was against one of the strongest sectors of the Moscow defence line and the

SS attack was brought to a halt by enfilading fire which forced the grenadiers to ground in the bed of a stream. SS artillery came up to engage its targets at point blank range, and by combining the fire of all the detachment's guns destroyed one strongpoint after another. As the Red infantry poured out of the positions which they had been holding the grenadiers rose to their feet and stormed Borisovo. Resistance had not been completely broken in all the areas along the regimental front and small parties of Soviet infantry and machine gunners forced the SS men to battle from house to house. In the bitter cold of 22 October the grenadiers of *Der Führer* regiment consolidated in the town of Borisovo and cleared the southern side in collaboration with Stukas of the Luftwaffe which crushed the last Red resistance. The rest of the day was spent concentrating the Division for new tasks which lay ahead. Moscow was now only 60 kms away.

Although Corps was to order further new advances up the Moscow highway it was clear that *Das Reich* Division had shot its bolt. The three weeks of campaigning had cost it over 400 killed, more than 5,500 wounded and nearly a thousand more missing and sick. For these heavy losses the grenadiers had carried the advance towards Moscow, the final objective of Army Group Centre, and had accomplished this under conditions of extreme privation. Due to the poor state of the roads there were days on which the grenadiers had had no hot food and few were the nights on which they had been quartered in warm and dry billets. They had not had a change of clothing, no winter equipment and often no change of socks for those worn since the beginning of the offensive.

Fighting against an enemy numerically superior, whose resistance had often had to be overcome in close combat, the SS men had thrust through carefully prepared lines of defence and had captured much booty and destroyed more, including 4 armoured trains.

On 26 October, the depleted Companies of grenadiers preparing to move out once again eastwards in new assaults were halted. Mud had bogged down the whole Corps and was to hold the vehicles fast in its grip until frost hardened the ground and allowed the German transport to move up the road which the grenadiers of the Waffen-SS had opened for them. We shall not, in this account, follow *Das Reich* Division into the resumption of 'Operation Typhoon', which was directed against Moscow and which was at first halted and then flung back by the Red Army. Our account ends here, with the exhausted grenadiers, after weeks of bitter fighting preparing themselves for new battles along the highway to Moscow.

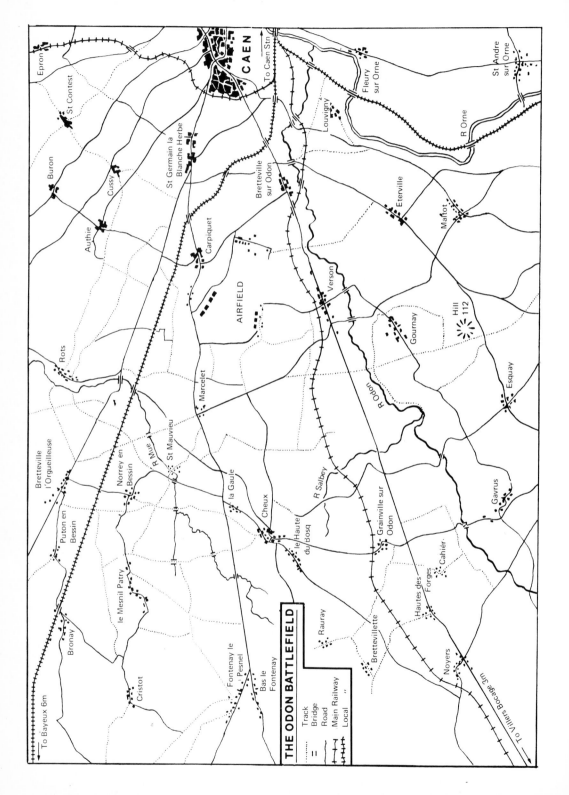

THE ODON BATTLEFIELD

Track		
Bridge		
Road		
Main Railway	"	
Local	"	

CAEN

To Caen Stn

To Bayeux 6m

Epron
St Contest
Buron
Cussy
St Germain la Blanche Herbe
Authie
Carpiquet
AIRFIELD
Rots
Marcelet
Bretteville l'Orgueilleuse
Norrey en Bessin
St Mauvieu
R Mue
la Gaule
Cheux
le Haute du Bosq
Puton en Bessin
le Mesnil Patry
Cristot
Fontenay le Pesnel
Bas le Fontenay
Bronay
Rauray
Bretteville sur Odon
Verson
R Odon
Gournay
Hill 112
Esquay
Gavrus
R Salbey
Grainville sur Odon
Hautes des Forges
Cahier
Brettevillette
Noyers
To Villers Bocage 8m
Louvigny
Fleury sur Orne
Eterville
Maltot
R Orne
St Andre sur Orne

12th Waffen-SS Division 'Hitler Jugend' in Normandy, June-July 1944

On 6 June 1944 the Western Allies debarked part of their armies upon the coast of Normady and thus began a campaign which was to recapture France, Belgium and parts of the Low Countries within months and which was, within a year, to play its part in the destruction of the Third Reich.

The greatest number of Allied soldiers who landed on D-Day and during the follow-up period were men untried in battle. Only a handful of Allied Divisions had been on active service, fighting in campaigns in the Mediterranean theatre of operations and these crack units served not only as the assault troops on D-Day but also acted as 'stiffeners' to the mass of highly trained but otherwise war-inexperienced formations.

In this account it is the men of the Canadian Army and of the 49th Infantry Division who, on the Allied side, bear the brunt of battle and most of these men, despite the years they had served in uniform, were unprepared for the savagery of the fighting in which they were to be engaged. Their principal enemy for the first month of the struggle in Normandy was a formation equally untried in battle, the 12th Waffen-SS Panzer Division *Hitler Jugend*. High on the roll of the accounts of military ability which were to be recorded during the fighting in the north-west European campaign must be the name of the 12th SS, the 'Hitler Youth' Division, for it emerged from the baptism of fire with a reputation for fighting ability and determination to win. Never on any battlefield of the Second World War were the words of Colonel du Picq to find their mark so truly. In his book *Etudes sur le Combat,* he wrote 'In a battle two moral forces, even more than two material forces, are in conflict. The stronger conquers. With equal or even inferior powers of destruction, he will win who is determined to advance'.

The 12th SS Panzer Division *HJ* was a very new division. When the order came to raise it veteran officers and NCO's of proved ability from the *Leibstandarte* were posted to the *HJ* and entrusted with the task of preparing for war a unit dedicated to the idea of combat pure and simple. To the great experience of warfare which their years on the Eastern Front had given these veterans was grafted the ruthless, almost fanatical desire of the young soldiers to fulfill the Will of their *Führer,* Adolf Hitler. Training was along lines unconventional by the

A camouflaged SdKfz 251/9 with a 7.5 cm gun.

standards of the day. There was no emphasis on drill or formal parades; every lesson and exercise had a purpose and had to be conducted as if the squad was undergoing battle conditions. Similar methods had been included in the standard SS training curriculum but in the 'HJ' Division training for battle was not merely the prime, but was indeed the only consideration. Thus, when the time came for its young soldiers to take their place in the battle line they were accustomed to being fired on with live ammunition, to barrages of real shell fire, to hunger, deprivation and to casualties. Even before their first battle these very young volunteers, almost boys—for their average age was so low that they were not allowed a cigarette ration but were issued with sweets and confectionary *in lieu* of tobacco—were mentally and physically prepared for the trials that lay ahead of them. If one adds to this high standard of training the advantages of controlled ruthlessness, bravery, experience and ideological indoctrination then the end product is the 'warrior', the man of war and it was such men who, for over a month, upset the plans of the British and Canadians and denied to them the strategically important city of Caen which had been among the first objectives planned to be taken after debarkation upon the Normandy coast.

In the months preceding D-Day the *HJ* Division, which had been held in reserve by the *Oberkommando der Wehrmacht* (the Armed Forces High Command), was moved to Beverloo in Belgium and from thence to Normandy where it took up a position about 50 miles behind the coast in an area between Elbeuf and Argentan. In position on the Channel coast was the Army's 716th Infantry Division, considered by Allied Intelligence officers to be of low calibre but which fought so well against the invaders that it delayed the initial onrush.

Tactically, the 12th SS Panzer Division *HJ*, was linked with the 1st Waffen-SS Panzer Division *Leibstandarte SS Adolf Hitler*, in the I SS Panzer Corps which, as part of the OKW reserve, could not be

A formation of SdKfz 251's awaiting orders to advance.

committed to action without authority from the Supreme Commander, Adolf Hitler. Therein lay, perhaps, the reason for the fact that no concerted counter-attack was undertaken by the Germans against the first landings for Hitler had been asleep and no one among his officers had had the courage to wake him and to ask for his authority to move the panzer divisions of the OKW reserve into an assault. Rapid committment of this reserve was vital in the first hours after the landings; each succeeding boat load of Allied soldiers reaching the beaches swung the balance against the defenders of Normandy.

Within hours of the first landings the German counter moves had begun. The I SS Panzer Corps received orders from 7th German Army that *HJ* was to swing westwards and to pass south of Caen and at a certain point west of that city it would come under the command of 84th Corps. From its positions around Lissieux which had been reached and occupied early in the afternoon of 6 June, the *HJ* was put under immediate notice to move and within two hours was ready to march and to carry out the orders '. . . in conjunction with *Panzer Lehr* Division to sweep west of Caen'.

Many writers when dealing with Waffen-SS Divisions have laid stress of the fact that these formations and particularly the Germanic Waffen-SS, enjoyed a higher establishment of vehicles, weapons and supplies than comparable Army units and that it was precisely this advantage in numbers which accounted for the successes which the SS obtained *vis-a-vis* those of the Army. This claim cannot be substantiated and, indeed, the reverse is more often the case for all supplies and equipment came through the Army Quartermaster's Department. The situation regarding rations for the *HJ* Division was somewhat unusual for it was found that the recruits were so undernourished when joining the regiments that supplements to the Army's ration scales had to be indented for. These additions to the rations ceased to be issued shortly after D-Day.

In the composition of units there was indeed a difference between SS and Army panzer formations. Each of the two Panzer grenadier regiments constituting the infantry component of an SS Panzer division contained three battalions instead of the two on the Army establishment. Only one of these three battalions was lifted in armoured personnel carriers; the other two battalions were brought forward in ordinary lorries. Each Grenadier regiment supported a panzer battalion one of which was made up of Panzer IV and the other Panzer V *Panther* vehicles. Much of the artillery was mechanised and the proportion of SP artillery in panzer divisions was quite high. In numbers the *HJ* Division was up to full strength with 20,540 all ranks but there were shortages of officers and it was understrength in armour having only 150 tanks instead of the 186 which was the full War establishment.

By the afternoon of 6 June authority had at last been received from Hitler allowing the OKW reserve forces to be committed to action and immediate preparation were made to launch a mass counter-attack against the British and Canadian forces which were moving inland from the beaches. Now that it had been released by Hitler's order the *HJ* roared forward, the fighting-fit grenadiers looking forward with confidence to their first taste of action, their induction into warrior-hood. By 16.00 hrs the two grenadier regiments had passed through Verson moving westwards towards the sound of the guns and,

A light Flak gun on a half-track and grenadiers of a panzer division on the Western Front, summer 1944.

unknowingly, on a collision course with 9th Canadian Brigade striking southwards from the beaches. During the short drive the *HJ* discovered that their training, however thorough, had been incomplete in certain things. During the advance through the open and undulating country the divisional lorried columns and armoured fighting vehicles had come under attack from fighter-bombers which swept down upon them in low level attacks. These and the bombardment by ship artillery from vessels firing miles away out to sea were new phenomena to both the veterans of Eastern Front and to the new recruits alike. After a certain period of confusion these assaults eventually became accepted as part of the new type of fighting which was being conducted in the West. Initially, however, the scale and fury of the first cannon and bomb assaults from Allied aircraft shook the young soldiers. Then they began to reply to the attacks opening fire upon the aeroplanes with rifles and machine guns. During this testing time the training which the drivers had been given proved itself for there was no bunching of vehicles and each driver so correctly maintained distance between himself and the machine ahead of him that casualties were reduced to a minimum.

Only after darkness had fallen did the fighter-bomber attacks cease and in the warm blackness of the early summer night the first vehicles of the Division crossed the Caen—Villers Bocage road and pressed onward into the unknown. The fog of battle had descended upon the Normandy battlefield and only scattered pieces of information were

Panzer grenadiers moving past a burning truck during the defensive fighting in Normandy in June-July 1944.

Panzer grenadiers go into battle supported by an assault gun armed with the long 7.5 cm gun.

A Waffen-SS panzer grenadier in action.

coming back from the bridgehead. From these it was clear that 716th Division holding the beach line had disintegrated and that there existed a gap through which the Canadian and British troops were thrusting and gaining ground. It was imperative that reliable, first-hand information be obtained about the strength and direction of the Allied drive for upon such Intelligence plans could be made to counter the thrust. Fritz Witt, commanding 12th SS Division, worked out a plan for a counter-attack to be launched which, in conjunction with 21st Panzer Division, would drive the Allies back into the sea. The divisional battle orders gave to the *HJ* grenadiers their objective—the beach. This mass attack would go in at midday on 7 June.

Throughout the night lorries bearing the grenadiers of *HJ* Division roared towards Caen but on the outskirts of the town they were forced to halt. There was no transport through the place for heavy bombardment had choked the streets with rubble and made them impassable to vehicles. There followed a night march under a barrage, through a seemingly dead city and, once clear of the burning streets the grenadiers of 25th Regiment, leading the advance, shook out into artillery formation and moved forward to their start lines. Artillery observation officers struck across country looking for high ground or for tall buildings from which they would direct the fire of their batteries during the coming battle. The bombing attacks had strung out the battalions and cohesion between them was lost. There was no longer an orderly, controlled move to designated positions but a hasty dash through unreconnoitred country towards a general area where the regiments would be concentrated. The units arrived in isolated lorries; a small group of infantry forced marching up the line, sometimes a small lorried group or a section of motorcyclists all intent upon reaching the battle zone.

As each grenadier Company arrived it was put hurriedly into position for now it was well into the night and the young men, who had been on the move since early morning, had much to do. Training paid its dividend, and with the ease of long familiarity the grenadiers dug their slit trenches, constructed simple dug-outs and excavated weapon pits for the 3.7 cm guns of the close support batteries. Then the anti-tank detachments came up, formed a gun line and quickly their weapons were in position, camouflaged and hidden from view under netting and leaves. With their defensive line dug and prepared the tired grenadiers could sleep for a few hours.

Miles behind them the armoured vehicles of their Panzer battalion were just beginning to move forward again having been halted by heavy Allied air attacks. Even with best possible speed it would not be able to reach the line in time to participate in the forthcoming offensive for only 50 of the Panzer IV's were with the grenadiers. Even more dramatic was the situation with the 26th Regiment for all its grenadier battalions and its Panther battalion were far removed from the battlefield. The tanks had run out of fuel 22 miles east of the Orne river and were stranded. There was no longer any possibility of a combined counter-attack; rather the fate of the Normandy front in the Caen sector depended principally upon three battalions of 25th Panzer Grenadier regiment who had been deployed to form a protective arc to the north and to the west of Caen. All three battalions were in the line:

1st was positioned on the right wing touching 21st Panzer Division. The 2nd Battalion was concentrated around St Contest and 3rd was on the left flank near the main Caen—Bayeux road. Two panzer detachments were deployed, one on the right wing and one on the left and the regimental artillery was placed south of Caen. This small force, well trained but without combat experience would be the first of the *HJ* Division to meet the Canadian blow, contain it and then without pause or let up drive into its own counter-attack and hope that its impetus would thrust the invaders back into the sea.

The Canadian presence was not long in making itself felt. The 9th Infantry Brigade was making its way southwards moving forward in the hope of extending the beachhead area and unaware that its advance guard was driving into an area recently occupied by the 'Hitler Youth' and that the flank which it was presenting to that Division was completely uncovered. Through the noise of the Allied bombardment and the myriad sounds of battle the grenadiers heard a new noise, that of tank engines as the first Stuarts of Canadian 27th Armoured Regiment's point unit rolled through the stone walled lanes which traverse the gently rolling countryside. The objective for the 9th Brigade was Franqueville and it was upon this target that the whole attention of the Canadians was directed. That the advance would take it across the front of a German unit facing westwards could not have been known to the Canadians although in their move from Buron to Authie they had been bombarded from St Contest, a village standing on higher ground than Buron. This fire had been so heavy that the armour had had to halt and the infantry had dispersed but even these signs of enemy watchfulness and first-class observation points had been insufficient to warn the 27th Armoured Regiment.

The drive through the grain fields and the fruit orchards which are a feature of the Normandy region of France had taken the point unit too far away from 1st battalion of 25th Panzer Grenadier regiment for that unit to have intervened effectively and thus it was across the front of 2nd battalion of that regiment, dug in near the line of the Caen—Bayeux road, that the Stuart tanks were passing. The thinly armoured flanks of 'A' Company's vehicles were presented as a target to a well concealed anti-tank gun line set up less than two hundred yards from the Canadian axis of advance.

The greatest danger with raw troops is that their excitement may cause them to open fire prematurely and thus alert the enemy but the fire discipline of the grenadiers was firm and they held their fire allowing the Canadian vehicles to roll past them. Then advancing from a reverse slope, across the crest of a low hill and then down the forward slope poured a wavelet of Panzer IV tanks taking the Stuarts under fire. The German anti-tank gun line opened up and as the artillery engaged the attention of the tank men grenadiers from 3rd battalion, using every dip and fold of the ground, raced forward to intercept the follow up infantry of 'C' Company the North Nova Scotia Highlanders and to prevent them supporting the tanks. The leading grenadiers stormed into Authie and, flinging a pincer movement around 'C' Company of the North Nova Scotias, thrust aside other groups from the Cameron Highlanders of Ottawa and the Sherbrooke Fusiliers, captured the village and overran 'A' Company of the Nova Scotias.

Panzer grenadiers enjoy a welcome rest next to a Tiger tank in a wood in summer 1944. Note the corrugated 'Zimmerit' mass covering the armour plating which largely reduced the effect of magnetic and hollow-charge anti-tank weapons.

While the point unit was thus engaged and fighting desperately the 1st and 2nd battalions of 25th SS Panzer Grenadier regiment flung themselves forward into the assault and bit deep in the flank of the 9th Brigade's advance.

Under the suddenness of the assault the leading troops of the Canadian Brigade began to give ground and, without pause, the storming grenadiers swept the Canadians back to their start lines at St Contest and at Buron. There was bitter fighting around this latter place and the Nova Scotias lost heavily trying to deny the little village to the Germans. The SS captured the place in the afternoon and then lost it to a Nova Scotia charge. By 17.00 hrs the fighting was general along the Canadian line of advance and the SS had shown their flexibility in each of the military roles which they had had to play. From a watching position to aggressive defence and then into a counter-attack; each phase of the battle closely followed the other. The Canadians who earlier in the day had had little artillery support could now offer complete coverage to their troops and a drum fire was poured down upon 3rd SS battalion at Buron. The 2nd battalion was heavily committed to fighting the Shermans and Stuart tanks at close quarters in and around the hamlet of St Contest. The whole line of the SS regiment had swung into a counter-attack pivoting on the right wing held by the 1st battalion and it appeared that the three battalions would eventually advance side by side in a general thrust to the coast. It

seemed as if nothing could halt the SS advance. A hail of gunfire poured down upon the battalions; concentrated barrages of artillery fire destroyed Buron as the Canadian gunners sought to achieve with shells that which neither superiority in tank numbers nor the Canadian infantry had been able to accomplish.

In time the advance did halt. It was ordered to halt for the right wing of the regiment was uncovered and 1st battalion was threatened with being outflanked. British armour had found this sensitive spot and by tank gunfire backed by artillery had caused confusion to the young grenadiers. The pace of 1st battalion advance hesitated and then began to halt. This was the time for personal example and Kurt Meyer, the officer commanding 25th Regiment, describes in his book *Gre-nadiere* how the battalion officers rallied and led their men forward again. Quickly an anti-tank gun line was set up and went into action destroying the Canadian vehicles which had come within range. The others faltered in their attack and at this sign of indecision a few Panzer IV's roared into a local counter-attack and restored the situation.

It had been a close thing and reflected the disastrous tactical situation in which 25th Grenadier Regiment had been placed. The unit was isolated and had both flanks uncovered. The right wing had lost touch with 21st Panzer Division and the 26th SS Regiment had still not arrived in its concentration area. To avoid the certainty of being surrounded and destroyed piecemeal the battalions of 25th Regiment were withdrawn to high ground and held there until the main of 26th Regiment came up. By dawn both regiments were in the line in strength.

But as the fighting died away on that first day the time had come to assess the losses and gains of 7 June. On the positive side the recruits had acquitted themselves with distinction. Losses had not been light; Scappini, commanding 2nd battalion, had been beheaded by a shell fired from a Sherbrooke Fusiliers tank as he led his men into action at St Contest and in that battalion, as well as in the other two, there had been losses among the junior officers. The panzer battalion had lost two Panzer IV's completely destroyed and four damaged but capable of being turned into 'runners' again. The Canadian 27th Armoured Regiment had had 28 cruiser tanks knocked out and infantry losses had exceeded three hundred. The greatest achievement had been, however, that the SS counter-attack had thrown back the Canadian spearhead for more than two miles and the ground which had been gained was to be held for nearly a month against major Allied assaults in strength.

In an attempt to 'blood' the 26th Grenadier Regiment and to achieve tactically more favourable positions the 1st and 2nd battalions of that regiment made a dawn attack upon Norrey and Putot driving out the Royal Winnipeg Rifles from their positions by the late afternoon. The Winnipeg Rifles regrouped and went in with a rush forcing the grenadiers back and by 21.30 hrs the village was again in Allied hands. The pressure which 7th Brigade was exerting upon 26th Regiment led to a relief attack being mounted by 25th Regiment

Waffen-SS panzer grenadier machine-gunners digging their fox-holes under enemy fire.

Assault guns and armoured personnel carriers of a battle group moving into action, 1944.

together with a Panther Company from 1st Panzer battalion. At last light the panzers advanced as a wedge and thrust towards Franqueville, along the Caen—Bayeux road. Each armoured vehicle carried groups of young grenadiers and accompanying the assault rolled a battery of 8.8 cm Flak guns, ready to give close and accurate support.

At the tiny hamlet of Rots there was a slight delay while the reconnaissance group had a short, fierce fire fight with the Canadian defenders. Then the village was free and the panzers passed through the narrow streets in single file, reformed on the far side and swung into attack formation ready to continue the drive for the next bound of the attack, Bretteville l'Orgueilleuse. Aware that the Canadians were now aroused it was decided to carry out the attack along the tactical principles which had been found to be most effective on the Eastern Front: the position would be rushed at top speed with all guns blazing. The tanks struck the village, the grenadiers flung themselves from the moving vehicles and engaged the Regina Rifles, whose tactical headquarters was in one of the village houses. Outside the village the guns of 3rd Anti-tank Regiment gave support to the Regina Rifles firing at the Panzer V's as they roared up and down the village street. Slowly the Rifles gave ground and in bursts of fierce fighting were forced back and out of the village. Once again the Canadians refused to accept defeat and hastily assembled groups rushed into the counter-attack which snatched back Bretteville from the grenadiers. Canadian riflemen fought with PIAT anti-tank weapons against the German armour and accounted for at least one of the six tanks destroyed in the fighting. The grenadiers withdrew.

This night fight marked a climax in the course of operations. Not for weeks were the Allies to advance any significant distance into the lines held by the *HJ* Division nor was that division to extend its own hold although many plans were put forward to reduce the Allied beachhead. The tide of events had turned decisively against the Germans in Normandy. They could now no longer mount an offensive that had any hope of driving the British and the Americans back into the sea. Now their task was to contain the Allied lodgement area, a task made more difficult with each succeeding day and to recover, by desperate counter-attack any position which was lost. The military equation was that to lose a foot of Normandy was worse than losing 10 miles of any other part of France. To ensure that Normandy would be held whole areas were sown with mines and booby traps and field defences of great strength were constructed. The SS lay secure behind the fortifications which they had erected, grimly determined to hold out. By the 16 June losses had been so great that the average SS battalion strength was that of two former Companies. Most of the junior officers had been killed and among the senior commanders who had fallen was Witt, the General Officer commanding the Division. The 12th SS was bleeding to death, for neither reinforcements of men nor replacements for the lost tanks had been received. Such was the weak state of the German Army in north west Europe that this fine panzer division, designed and armed for aggressive, mobile warfare was used in a static defensive role.

On 17 June a new British unit was put into the line against the *HJ* Division. The 49th Infantry Division was given the task of pressing the attack southwards and to secure good tactical points for the eventual seizure of Caen. At 14.00 hrs of 17 June the 6th battalion the Duke of Wellington's Regiment was ordered to capture the Boislande park dominated by its *chateau*. For this assault four regiments of Field artillery, supported by independent mortar batteries, bombarded the SS trench line along the western edge of the park. Three thousand shells fell upon the positions held by No. 10 Company of 26th Grenadier Regiment's 3rd battalion and close behind the barrage rolled the Shermans of 24th Lancers.

The wave of fire and steel poured over the main positions held by No. 10 Company but small groups of grenadiers continued the fight from fox holes and shell craters, engaging the tanks and the follow up infantry with *Panzerfaust* rocket shells and sub-machine-guns. The drive by the West Riding Regiment swept forward and soon the isolated pockets of SS men fell silent. But not all the grenadiers had been killed for one of their principal and most efficient tactics was to remain in their trenches and not to withdraw unless they were directly attacked. Thus the assault would roll past them and then they would go to ground to emerge later to snipe or to attack sentry posts and thus create confusion in the enemy rear.

Soon the park had been cleared but the losses to 6th Duke of Wellington's had been severe. Fifty five killed and one hundred and ten wounded was the price of this engagement. All through the short June night the British infantry held position and in the early dawn of 18 June, Waterloo Day, began preparations to renew the attack to capture the village hard by the park, and which was held by No. 9 *HJ* Company. These preparations were halted by a well directed barrage which fell upon their positions forcing the West Riding Regiment to go

to ground. By early afternoon this bombardment had risen to a hurricane of fire. Under cover of this shell fire No. 9 Company made up its own assault from its trenches along the southern end of the wood. The Company commander, believing that attack should be met with attack led his grenadiers forward, their numbers being added to as other SS troopers from the overrun No. 10 Company emerged from hiding. A few SP guns rolled forward in support and some Panthers crashed through the thick undergrowth, adding weight to the counter-attack. Under the pressure of this furious assault 6th battalion was forced back to its start line with a loss of a further 30 dead and as many wounded.

The 7th battalion of the Duke of Wellington's Regiment was immediately sent in to take the park, a task which they accomplished against resistance so fanatical in its intensity that it left them too exhausted to carry the advance into the village of Boislande and they stayed holding the ground which they had won until 22 June. But the grenadiers had had to be withdrawn back to the village of Fontenoy which was held against probing attacks by the infantry battalions of 49th Division.

The direction of these thrusts then changed and one probe found the right wing boundary with *Panzer Lehr* Division and began to drive along this seam. Along this poorly defended sector British assaults were made to exploit the weakness. Thus on 18 June while the West Riding Regiment was assaulting Boislande other units of 49th Division mounted classic, set piece attacks against the villages of Christot and Fontenoy and, once again, the fully fury of the thrust came in against 3rd battalion of 26th Grenadier Regiment. The artillery barrage upon Fontenay not only destroyed all communication between the garrison and the outlying companies but annihilated group after group of the 'Hitler Youth' regiment. The officers and NCO's moved round the trench lines, encouraging their men and exposing themselves to the British artillery fire. The losses among the leaders left many units commanded only by grenadiers and without officers, often without NCO's of any rank. The small groups of young SS men fought back, with *Panzerfausts* against tanks, holding on until the Panzer Company could begin a counter-attack. Then together with the Panthers the exhausted grenadiers would make another effort to hold back the British advance. Losses on both sides were heavy and pillars of smoke marked the places where Allied and German tanks had been 'brewed up', but somehow the small groups of SS were regrouped and the line was held. But nearer to Caen *Panzer Lehr* Division had had to give ground and the situation for 3rd battalion became critical as the danger of being outflanked grew. The losses which that battalion had suffered in the bitter fighting since 18 June had been such that it had to be taken out of the line and the desperately tired groups of grenadiers marched back to rest positions.

By now the Allied bridgehead had been built up and reinforced to such a degree that more and more fresh troops could be put in to wear down the *HJ* defenders. The time had come for the Allies to burst out of the narrow confines of the lodgement area. Seeking to find a weak point along the front of 12th SS Division the British 30th Corps intended to capture the Rauray spur and the village dominating that feature. Corps decided to carry the advance from the positions held by the Duke of Wellington's regiment and that unit was relieved by 11th Durham Light Infantry who prepared themselves for the offensive. In the misty dawn of 26 June the watchful observation officers of the SS artillery saw the British armour concentrating for the assault and in burst of savage fire the barrages which they called down destroyed seven tanks and two SP guns. At midday the Durhams went into a two company attack, both companies going in with the bayonet. The Light Infantry poured from the Boislande woods with their trees stripped of foliage, down the forward slope of the hill, past the dead cattle putrefying in the summer heat and advanced upon the village of Rauray. There were fought battles of unusual ferocity and the struggle

An assault gun commander in summer camouflage dress. Note the throat microphones and communication control box.

was house to house, often room to room as the grenadiers sought to reduce the British advantages in armour by fortifying the buildings. From doors and windows, from gardens and from the cover of the stone walls which line the roads of this part of Normandy, the few SS soldiers, by now veteran survivors of the full-strength regiments which had entered the battle only weeks before, fired their rocket launchers at the British armour. Clouds of black smoke rising from the fields and streets of Rauray marked the 'kills' which they achieved in their bitter and lonely battles. But then the Division's Panthers together with armoured fighting vehicles from 2nd Panzer Division entered the fight and flung themselves at the British tanks.

The SS made the Durhams pay a high price for the ruins of Rauray and two hundred Light Infantrymen were killed or wounded in the battle. At last light both sides were exhausted and the fighting died away. Around Rauray there was to be a period of a few days during which there was little but patrol activity.

Following upon the 30th Corps attack it was the turn of British 8th Corps to take up the main effort once again and it was to make its thrust across the front held by 3rd Canadian Division, and to strike for the Odon river. During the fighting which then ensued the *HJ* Division's Engineer battalion holding post at Cheux was overrun by 15th Scottish Division and the Fife and Forfar Yeomanry, having beaten down the gun line and rolled over the anti-tank battalion. Only batteries of *Nebelwerfer* rocket projectors rushed from I SS Panzer Corps reserve were able to halt a complete breakthrough. Again the 26th Panzer Grenadier regiment became the focus of the British attack and against this new assault there was no hope of sustained defence for the whole divisional reserve had been committed.

Verson then became the key point which had to be held at all costs. The order went out to the exhausted grenadiers. The battered and hungry remnants of three battalions, tired and soaked from the rain which poured incessantly over the battlefield were told that the ground which they had held through weeks of battle as a springboard for an advance had now become a bastion which must be defended to the last round. And against this unyielding rock smashed a force of British infantry and armour—estimated by the Germans to have exceeded five hundred combat vehicles. Still the grenadiers fought on. Their orders were to hold until relieved by the fresh troops of II SS Corps whose arrival was anticipated within days. Even with their forward zones overrun and their main line under constant and increasing pressure they maintained the battle. They had always been inferior in number but the daily casualty wastage in men and vehicles had caused them to be hopelessly outnumbered. Once again the tactics of the Easter front proved themselves. Against any attack the SS infantry or panzer defenders would hold their fire until almost point-blank range so that the first shots would obtain a 'kill'. Then, before the British artillery could range in and bombard the position, a new location would be chosen and fire opened from a fresh direction. These tactics, used by both grenadiers and panzer men alike, reduced the British superiority in numbers and caused them to believe that the defenders were more numerous than they really were.

Weary panzer grenadiers move up past a Tiger tank.

A fresh crisis arose when a group of tanks from 11th British Armoured Division broke through the divisional front and brought not only the Support Company but also the divisional headquarters under fire. Fierce close combat battles were fought as the grenadiers attacked the British armour with rocket launchers. One group of tanks thrusting forward with grim determination knocked out a Panzer IV and then the lead Sherman was itself destroyed. Two more pressed forward the assault until *Panzerfausts* hit and destroyed them. Other British tank squadrons carried the advance forward. The last remaining SS anti-tank gun was hit and destroyed and the British tanks rolled forward over the Grenadier line. Rising from their slit trenches the *HJ* soldiers rushed forward to attack the armoured vehicles but were engaged by the British infantry following behind the machines. A hand to hand battle developed with the tanks firing at every sort of target and making ground until a Tiger tank rolled forward and beat them off.

The British thrust carried on flowing round pockets of fanatical resistance and reached the batteries of the SS artillery line. A single

Panzer IV drove forward trying to hold them back. Darkness fell but throughout the night the British probing attacks came in and bitter little fights flickered and burst into flame along the whole *HJ* front. At first light the battle flared again and continued until by 09.00 hrs no less than four separate and heavy assaults had been beaten off. At Grainville, during that morning a few panzers were hastily brought together and flung into a counter-attack to restore the position but their charge collapsed and failed in the defensive fire of a British gun line. On the Division's left flank a barrage fired from 600 guns crashed onto the German lines and Allied armour, storming close behind the shells, overran the SS forward positions.

Rauray, that hotly defended village, was finally lost to the Durham Light Infantry. British command of the air had so strangled the German lorried convoy system that shells were no longer reaching the artillery and against this weak opposition 8th Corps forced a bridgehead across the Odon river at Buron. The danger was now that Caen would be cut off from the south for 8th Corps proposed, in an operation codenamed 'Epson', to pass 11th Armoured division across the Odon river, to reach Point 112 and to cut the south-west road from Caen.

Point 112, a flat-topped hill, although low, dominated the sur-rounding countryside and was, therefore, of importance. By the afternoon of 27 June two armoured regiments of 11th Armoured Division were approaching the feature. In the early afternoon of 28 June, 'H' Company of 8th Battalion The Rifle Brigade, supported by two squadrons of 23rd Hussars stormed and captured the northern slopes of the hill.

The inevitable counter-attack came in mounted by 25th Grenadier Regiment's panzer battalion, reduced in numbers to the strength of a weak Company. Moving the point of the thrust from flank to flank, switching the direction of their attack from one area to another the panzers and their escorting 8.8 cm guns picked off the vehicles of 29th Armoured Brigade and, covered by artillery fire from Carpiquet and by mortar fire from Esquay, the grenadiers and their supporting tanks struck at and drove back from the summit of the hill the British riflemen and Hussars.

This counter-attack was part of the general one ordered by Hitler with the now hopeless task of destroying the Allied hold on Normandy. Thus on 29 June the last Battle for Caen opened and the British reply to the German break out attempt was to saturate the whole line from Verson to Point 112 with a storm of artillery fire. Once again the rifle Brigade and the Hussars attacked the flanks of Point 112 and once again they were driven from it. Point 112 was indefensible. Neither side could hold it and it was the SS which dominated the hill by artillery fire denying it to the British. After two unsuccessful assaults the 8th Corps offensive 'Operation Epsom' ended. The 12th SS Division *HJ* had saved Caen once again. Along other parts of the divisional battle line the assaults by little groups of exhausted grenadiers had met with little success. The Company in front of Rauray moved forward and

A flame-thrower detachment mounting a 'Zimmerit'-covered Panther tank during the fighting in Normandy, June 1944.

located the boundary between 8th and 30th Corps and caused, with their probing attacks, so much concern that 8th Armoured Brigade had to be brought up to defend the ground.

West of Caen the aerodrome at Carpiquet was defended by a small group of grenadiers, the last survivors of a company of 1st Battalion 26th Regiment. These 50 men held the hangars on the western side of the drome and to the west of the field the remnants of the battalion, one hundred men in all, were in a defensive position in the administration buildings. The only support for this desperate contingent reposed in a few 8.8 cm flak guns, a handful of tanks and little else. There were no other heavy weapons nor any sort of reserves. Against this little group of defenders air assaults were launched, followed by naval bombardments. A complete Army Group Artillery force fired barrages to prepare the ground for the attacks which 3rd Canadian Division was to mount.

The Canadian attack was imposing in its strength. The whole of 8th Infantry Brigade together with the Royal Winnipeg Rifles from 7th Brigade was to make the infantry assault and in support of that drive would be 10th Armoured Regiment backed up by some of the special tanks from 79th Armoured Division. Twelve batteries of Field artillery, eight of Medium and one Heavy regiment were to crush the enemy with shell fire and overhead two Squadrons of Typhoons would beat down the opposition with rocket fire.

At 06.00 hrs on 4 July the assault opened and the Winnipeg Rifles advanced to the attack out of the village of Marcellt. The German defenders had improved the positions which had been hastily dug weeks before and had extensive fields of fire. The Canadian armour had to advance across ground as flat as a billiard table and as the vehicles emerged from the woods the defensive fire pattern was poured upon them. Then the few panzers available were flung into the attack and under this double assault the Canadian thrust halted and then fell back. The Canadian infantry, too, had to cross the open space of the airfield and suffered terrible losses as they moved towards the hangars and the men who defended them. The village of Carpiquet was taken but the assault on the buildings by the Winnipeg Rifles failed. Losses on both sides had been heavy; the SS garrison was now reduced to 20 men; not one of them an NCO or an officer. Nevertheless, this little band carried out a counter-attack during the night and made some progress but, being too weak in numbers to hold the ground which they had won, had to return to their former positions. This aggressive thrust carried out during the night of 5th July, kept the Canadians on that sector on the defensive for the remainder of the battle. The grenadiers held their posts until 8 July and the Canadian losses were alarming. The North Shore Regiment had lost 132, as had the Winnipeg Rifles; The Queen's Own Rifles of Canada had lost 26, the Regiment Chaudiere 57 and Armoured regiment 20 men.

Despite orders from Hitler that Caen was to be held to the last it was clear that the *HJ* positions around the town were now untenable. The divisional commander Meyer asked for permission to evacuate the town and thereby to save the depleted regiments from total annihilation. Until the reply was received from Hitler's headquarters the battle still had to be fought and at the height of the fierce fighting the unit on right flank of *HJ* Division gave ground. Through this gap poured two more British divisions. To counter this thrust and to restore the situation *HJ* moved the last vehicles from its depleted panzer battalions to the threatened flank. By now there were no Company officers with either 1st or 2nd battalions of 25th Grenadier Regiment and the anti-tank guns of 2nd battalion had all been destroyed. The 3rd battalion was still holding on to the ruins of Buron, fighting back the attacks by the Highland Light Infantry of Canada. That battalion lost 262 of its men battling for the village but then it broke through and pushed the advance to St Contest. Panzers from 2nd battalion rolled forward against the tanks of 27th Armoured Regiment but failed to

Waffen-SS panzer grenadiers in Normandy, summer 1944.

Waffen-SS motorised troops during a break in the fighting.

recapture the village. In quick succession Canadian blows along the 3rd Division front achieved gains. At Guchy the 25th Grenadier Regiment lost its No. 6 Company which was rolled over by the Canadian armour. Only one grenadier escaped. Authie fell to the North Nova Scotia Highlanders and then Franqueville was lost but against each of these Canadian thrusts the grenadiers flung counter attacks, delaying but never halting the Allied advance. The situation already critical became hopeless as the unceasing Allied blows threatened to tear the Division apart. Only the loosest cohesion existed between the units of the *HJ* Division; isolated groups fighting bitter battles against overwhelming odds. The 3rd battalion of 25th Grenadier Regiment had lost most of its men in Buron but the Highland Light Infantry of Canada had lost half a battalion, and the SS resistance was not crushed until flame-throwing tanks incinerated the last defenders. North of St Contest No. 15 Panzer Company sent in its last tanks against the Shermans storming down on the village. Attempts by the Canadians to win ground around Authie were held back by a scratch force of Panthers, and at Cussy the gunners of a battery of 8.8 cm flak guns died at their posts.

'Operation Charnwood', the capture of Caen, opened on 8 July and everywhere the pressure against 12th SS Division grew in intensity. The Regina Rifles attacked the tactical headquarters of 25th Panzer Grenadier regiment in the Abbey of Ardenne, striking forward through the disintegrating defences. Once again the story was repeated; a handful of men hastily assembled from a grenadier battalion, together with a Company of *HJ* Panther tanks and panzer grenadiers from the *Leibstandarte SS Adolf Hitler*, struck back at the advancing Allies and halted their advance. During the night the last troops were withdraw from the abbey.

The end was not far off. The infantry strength of 12th SS was down to that of one battalion—the equivalent of five battalions had been destroyed in the fighting. Most close support weapons had been destroyed as had most of the anti-tank guns. Batteries of field artillery had been overrun and remaining batteries were down to one or two weapons. The losses in armoured fighting vehicles had been calamitous; only 65 remained, this representing well over a fifty per cent loss. There was no longer any point in the sacrifice of any more soldiers and Division, without reference to I SS Panzer Corps, ordered that Caen be given up. With communications so bad this message was not received by all units and some remained in position holding out and fighting to the last. The remnants of 25th Grenadier Regiment's 1st battalion continued to resist until it was destroyed by fighter bomber attack.

By midday of 9 July the last exhausted grenadiers of the 'Hitler Youth' Division had crossed the Orne river immediately followed by SS Engineers who blew the river bridges. Behind them the panzer grenadiers of the 12th SS left not only their many dead, for the Division had suffered a 60% casualty rate (20% killed and 40% wounded), but also a reputation for bravery that was to be acknowledged by one Canadian historian with the following words: 'The 12th SS which defended this sector (of Normandy) fought with a toughness and a determination which was never to be met with at any time again during the (north west European) campaign'.

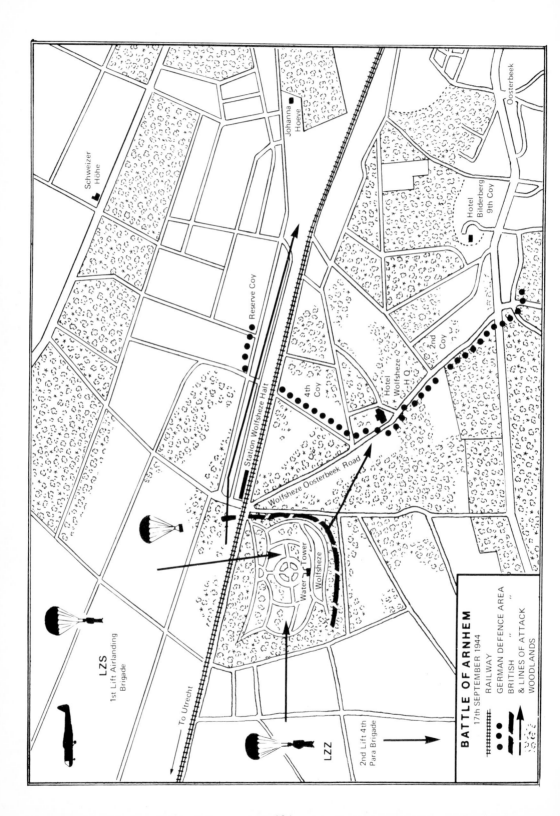

BATTLE OF ARNHEM
17th SEPTEMBER 1944

RAILWAY
GERMAN DEFENCE AREA
BRITISH "   "
& LINES OF ATTACK
WOODLANDS

LZS
1st Lift Airlanding
Brigade

LZZ
2nd Lift 4th
Para Brigade

To Utrecht

Schweizer
Höhe

Johanna
Hoeve

Reserve Coy

Station Wolfsheze Halt

4th
Coy

Wolfsheze Oosterbeek Road

Water Tower

Wolfsheze

Hotel
Wolfsheze
HQ

2nd
Coy

Hotel
Bilderberg
9th Coy

Oosterbeek

104

16th Waffen-SS Training and Replacement Battalion: Its First Day of Battle Against the British Airborne Troops near Arnhem, September 1944

On 17 September, 1944, by a tragic and unforseeable coincidence, the air drop and glider landing zones of part of 1st British Airborne Division were laid out within a mile of an area controlled by Panzer Grenadier Companies of an SS battalion, whose front covered three of the principal axes of advance upon the airborne objectives inside the town of Arnhem.

The week long battle which followed the airborne assault has passed into history as the battle of Arnhem, but it is with the fighting of the first day that we are concerned and, particularly, with the part played by those SS Panzer Grenadier companies. Some of the men of those formations were 19-year-old boys while others were men convalescent and, therefore, unfit for active service. And yet, to some degree, the fighting ability of those men was, perhaps, instrumental in destroying the British paratroop advances and nullifying a strategic thrust which might have ended the war during the Autumn of 1944.

The military situation for the Germans in the weeks up to the end of August 1944 was that its Army was in full and complete retreat northwards and eastwards towards the frontier. In the three months of June, July and August it had suffered a loss equivalent to that of 53 Divisions of men—no less than 300,000 in killed, wounded and captured. In August, although the German forces facing the Western Allies still totalled 48 infantry and 15 Panzer divisions, this was a paper potential for these were all understrength formations whose total numbers were not equal to that of 27 standard divisions. Against them the Allies could field 49 first class divisions and had the German troops all been of good fighting quality then the disparity between their strength and that of the Allies might not have been so alarming to OKW. But a large number of the German battalions, regiments and even divisions was made up of men with illnesses which, in other times, would have excluded them from military service. There were, for example, whole battalions of men with stomach ulcers who needed a special diet, and other units whose soldiers had disabilities equally as serious. It was, therefore, not a first-class fighting army which confronted the Americans as they drove eastwards towards the Rhine or the British as they advanced triumphantly northwards through Belgium, crossing those battlefields on which their fathers had fought during the four bitter years of the First World War.

In desperation Hitler recalled to command Field Marshal von Runstedt, whom he had dismissed after the collapse in Normandy, and the veteran Prussian soldier took up post on 4 September. One day later the battered remnants of the Germany Army in the West crossed from Belgium into Holland, their appearance giving conviction to the Dutch people that this was a beaten force anxious only to get home. Some idea of the state of the German Army at that time must have been known to General Montgomery for he proposed to the Supreme Commander, Eisenhower, the daring plan to lay a 64 mile long carpet of airborne soldiers through Holland to Arnhem, in which town they would take and hold a bridgehead across the Rhine. To carry out this task the airborne troops would have to seize a series of crossings, five of which would be of important bridges across three rivers, and to hold open a corridor while British armour struck along it and through it into the North German plain.

Young Waffen-SS panzer grenadiers moving up to the line on foot and by carrier.

Once Eisenhower had accepted the plan work went ahead for an operation involving a whole allied airborne army, but we are concerned here only with Lathbury's 1st Para Brigade whose task it would be to land and to dash for the Arnhem bridges. The brigade was made up of three battalions: Dobie's 1st, codenamed Leopard whose task it was to drive down the main Ede—Arnhem road and occupy the high ground to the north of the city. Frost's 2nd battalion codenamed Lion, would advance along a secondary road close to the north bank of the Rhine and would capture the main railway bridge, while Fitch's 3rd battalion, codenamed Tiger, would thrust down the Utrecht—Arnhem road and by approaching the bridge from the north would not only cover but reinforce Frost's battalion in its task.

From the map it can be seen that the British drop and landing zones were located some way outside Arnhem, because Allied intelligence officers had forecast that there would be unacceptably high casualties from flak if the drops were made on or near the bridge. Thus it was vital to the success of the plan that the British airborne men move without delay and with maximum speed to cover the 10 kms from the landing zones to their objectives in the town. It was known that certain SS armoured formations were in the area but their threat was minimised and Allied intelligence seemed unaware that under von Runstedt's firm grip the German retreat had ended and that the Army was not only pulling itself together but was flinging units southwards to meet and to delay the onrushing British armour.

As part of Runstedt's measures an *ad-hoc* German division commanded by General von Tettau had begun to build a defence line in central Holland, and one of the divisional units was 16th Waffen-SS Replacement and Training battalion. Early in September certain Grenadier companies from that battalion, together with a headquarters group, had been detached and put into divisional reserve just outside Arnhem. The strength of this small group, named 'Battalion Krafft' after its 37-year-old commander, was 12 officers, 65 NCOs and 229 men. In view of the possibility of Allied airborne operations the tasks of the divisional reserve were to combat air landings, to guard the Rhine crossings at Arnhem and to prepare the bridges for demolition should a *coup de main* be made against them.

The new commander of Army Group B, Field Marshal Model, established his headquarters in the hotel in which the SS battalion had been billeted, and the Panzer Grenadier companies were moved out to another suburb, Wolfsheze, in whose principal hotel Krafft set up his headquarters. It was in the Wolfsheze area and across the roads leading into Arnhem that the men of 16th SS battalion were deployed.

In the morning of Sunday 17 September, 1944, the intensity of the air raids on Arnhem and its suburbs indicated that some sort of attack was under way. Krafft put his battalion on immediate alert, and shortly thereafter the first British landings were reported.

The SS commander ordered patrols out to establish how strong the British were, whether the airborne troops were motorised and also the direction in which they were moving. In addition No. 9 Company, which was in Arnhem, was ordered forward and No. 2 Company, holding the ground adjacent to the drop zones was sent into the attack.

Patrols from No. 2 Company were out within minutes of the first landings and behind these the main of the Company moved up to the edge of the Wolfzele woods from the cover of whose trees they opened fire upon the paratroopers falling from the sky and on the gliders as they careered across the fields only yards from the muzzles of their guns. The flimsy walls of the gliders were no protection from the machine gun bullets, and the MG platoon of No. 2 Company jubilantly reported how they had destroyed four of the gliders skidding over the grass. No British soldier had emerged from the shot-up wrecks. But the Airborne men were skilled in war and within minutes their aggressive patrols had forced the SS Grenadiers and the machine gun groups to withdraw from the drop zone. Deep in the woods of Wolfszele the men of No. 2 Company set up a battle line and prepared to hold this until No. 4 Company, the headquarters detachment and No. 9 Company arrived in the battle area to hold the British advance.

Krafft was puzzled. As a trained soldier he could not determine what objective it was that the British intended to capture. He reasoned that it was unlikely to be the headquarters of Army Group 'B', nor even an attempt to seize the airfied at Deelen. The only other strategic target was the giant railway bridge in Arnhem but the landings had been made so far distant from the town that even this seemed an unlikely target. But whatever the objective was the patrol reports showed that the British were preparing to move into the city. Krafft made his own

Panzer grenadiers aboard their armoured personnel carrier. The open superstructure left the men very vulnerable to shell fire although the angled armoured sides of the vehicle gave protection against shell splinters and small arms fire.

A StuG III assault gun armed with the long 7.5 cm gun on the way to the front.

reconnaissance and appreciation of the situation. From these he estimated that between 3,000 and 4,000 men had been landed, that these had assembled west of the Wolfsheze road and that they were preparing to drive southwards. Immediately he swung his line to form along the Wolfsheze—Oosterbeek road between the railway in the north and the Utrecht road in the south. The No. 4 Company was placed on the right wing and to protect its flank the reserve platoon was placed north of the railway line. No. 2 Company was on the left, with its left wing bent backwards to guard the flank. Machine guns formed the corner stones of his defence and platoons of these were posted to either end of the line while his Grenadiers dug in in the thick woods through which the British would have to pass. Krafft was determined that even if he could not halt the British advance indefinitely at least his defence would force the paratroops to undertake a long diversion. To bolster his thin line of Grenadiers he brought up the battalion's heavy weapons units. Two anti-tank guns were sited on the Wolfsheze road near the Hotel Wolfsheze which Krafft used as his Tac HQ, and another gun was set on a road junction to guard No. 2 Company's left wing. The anti-aircraft guns were sited around the hotel and to the south of the HQ building were the mortars. In addition to the standard 81 mm pieces Krafft's battalion had also received a group of experimental large-calibre rocket mortars.

Placed where they were the mortar detachments would be able to engage targets along the whole length of the battalion sector.

The speed of reaction on the German side was proof of the excellence of the training which was given, for within minutes of the first landings being reported a plan had been decided upon, the airborne troops had been attacked and a battle line had been drawn up. Within a few hours this line had been thickened by the arrival of No. 9 Company which went into reserve positions and increased the battalion strength to 13 officers, 73 NCOs and 349 men. With the line established men from each Company were detached to form a counter attack reserve and the SS men were told that by constant aggression the British would be unsettled and deceived as to the strength of the troops facing them. They were also aware that no reinforcements could be expected to arrive before the evening and that the battalion's task was, therefore, to delay the British. All ranks were aware of the task confronting them. Against the 4,000 highly trained elite airborne troops Krafft was intending to fling his 300 young soldiers and convalescents and certainly he did not expect to see the end of that day. Nevertheless he showed optimism in his radio messages, particularly in that to Division in which he stated his intention of mounting a night attack. Division ordered him instead to move towards the town of Wolfsheze to interrupt the British move from north to south.

The descents by both 1st British Para Brigade and 1st Air Landing Brigade had been overwhelmingly successful and the initial confusion had been overcome. The advance began towards the objectives and Urquhart urged on his men to cover the ten kilometres to the bridges. But delays were already being experienced. The Dutch population, yearning to be free and influenced by the dispirited showing of the German troops as these had retreated through the town only weeks before, thought that the war was over and lavished their hospitality upon the airborne soldiers. Accompanied by cheering civilians the thin line of camouflage-smocked warriors swung down the roads marching, unknown to them, towards the battle line which Krafft had set up. First contact was made at about 16.00 hrs and the temperamental wireless sets once again bedevilled communications on both sides. Krafft was convinced that he was surrounded, while the British could not establish either the length of the German defensive line nor the strength in which it was held.

One of the first casualties in the SS sector was General Kussin, the Arnhem Field Commander, who arrived in the battalion area on a tour of inspection and who had insisted upon leaving by that road along which he had driven up to the Wolfsheze hotel. A para patrol from 3rd battalion reached the junction of the Wolfsheze—Doorwerth roads and took under fire the General's camouflaged civilian car as it roared towards them. The occupants were all killed.

British pressure upon No. 2 Company forced the SS Grenadiers back from the crossroads, but MG fire and snipers in the trees extracted from the airborne men a heavy blood price for each yard of ground which they gained. Krafft knew that the crossroads were vital to his defence and bringing No. 9 Company out of reserve launched it, together with an SP gun, into an attack to retake the road junction. To support this vital assault the mortars were ordered to lay a barrage, an

A panzer grenadier machine-gunner firing his MG 42.

anti-tank gun was brought forward and No. 2 Company gave up a heavy machine gun group. Then from reports received from No. 4 Company on the right flank it was clear that the direction of the British attack was about to change again, and that another main effort would be made against the left flank. Krafft decided to destroy this by using his rocket mortars and ordered the battery commander to open fire with his 28 cm and 32 cm high explosive and incendiary projectiles upon the British forming-up area around Wolfsheze.

Despite this support the attack by No. 9 Company made no ground but it had diverted and tied down the airborne men, preventing them from advancing towards the town. Bitter, close range warfare, much of it hand to hand fighting developed along the whole of the German line but the forces were so strongly matched in courage that neither could prevail against the other and force it to quit the field. The British build-up had however allowed the paras to extend their flank so that this overlapped the SS wing and they began to infiltrate past the turned flank and move towards the objectives. Slowly the SS Company began to be forced back from its positions along the road. Other airborne thrusts had also reached the railway line, cutting the SS battalion off

A Waffen-SS panzer grenadier in typical summer camouflage smock.

almost completely. Frost's 2nd battalion swung further out, past the SS flank and moved on their line of advance along the river bank but then, en route, struck and were held temporarily by the SS group whose task it was to secure the ferry crossings across the Rhine.

It was now clear that although Arnhem was the British objective this could not be taken until the SS battalion obstructing the advance had been destroyed or driven back. Krafft was as determined as ever to hold his position for as long as daylight lasted but intended, once darkness had set in, to slip his men out of the encirclement and regain the German main positions. He could not know for certain, although he may have expected it, that the German forces had reacted quickly to the British airdrop and had brought into action strong forces including 9th and 10th SS Divisions of II SS Panzer Corps which were rearming and reforming nearby.

For the remainder of the day the battle pattern remained almost unchanged. British thrusts were met with German counter thrusts. An airborne push in one sector was counter-attacked by a Grenadier drive in another. The close quarter battle swayed backwards and forwards across a very thin strip of ground and along a very short front. The drive by 3rd para battalion around the SS battalion's left wing now posed a very serious threat and the mortar detachments in an effort to drive back the aggressive British troopers fired no fewer than 750 shells. The fury of this bombardment concentrated within a short space of time and a small area halted, but only temporarily, the British drive on No. 2 Company's area but to the north No. 4 Company reported that there was the sound of small arms fire 2 kms behind them and it was clear that the infiltrating paratroops had encircled the battalion.

Krafft issued break-out orders emphasising that until the time came to disengage from the British the line had to be held. The break out would be made to the east and would be led by a point unit made up of a platoon from No. 2 Company backed up by the SP gun and two anti-tank guns. The main force would be made up of the remainder of No. 2 Company, the headquarters group, the heavy weapons, and the remaining two Companies, each minus one platoon. The platoons from No. 4 and from No. 9 Companies, together with an anti-tank gun, formed the rear guard. All wounded were loaded on the transport together with spare weapons and equipment, while all unusable equipment and broken down lorries were destroyed.

From 22.00 hrs the units withdrew from the perimeter by platoons; small groups of Grenadiers moving stealthily through the dark forests. Within half an hour the survivors of the battalion had concentrated and the convoy moved off, the vehicles lit only briefly in the light of the briskly burning ammunition trucks, victims of the afternoon battle. An hour later the column had passed up the highway, reached the Arnhem—Ede crossroads just outside Arnhem and linked up with SS Division *Hohenstaufen's* Battle Group Spindler, under which command Krafft placed himself and his group. The 16th Waffen-SS Training and Replacement battalion's first day of battle had ended.

In a report to Himmler Krafft praised the bravery and endurance of his men who had acquitted themselves like veterans. Whether, as has been claimed for the Panzer Grenadiers, the delay caused to the British by the SS battalion was the main cause of the failure by the Airborne Division to reach its objectives is, of course, open to dispute. But what is not in doubt is the bravery and determination of the Grenadiers in taking on an enemy far superior in numbers to themselves, and by an exhibition of soldierly qualities impeding his advance.

It may well be the case that Krafft's battalion on Sunday 17 September, 1944, occupying as it did important ground dominating three main approaches into Arnhem, converted its tactical situation into a strategic role by gaining time for the Germans to form a strong defensive line, and that this prevented the establishing of a bridgehead across the Rhine from which the death thrust to Hitler's Third Reich might have been made and the European war brought to its end in the Autumn of 1944.

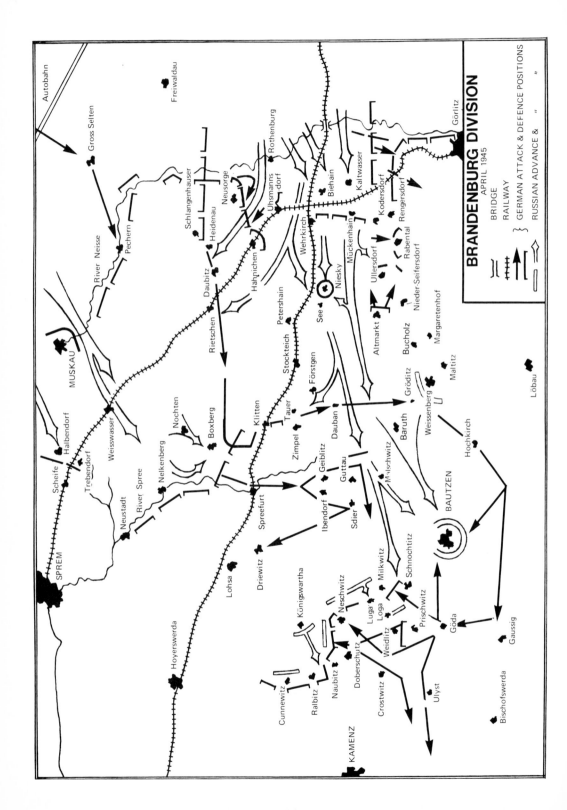

BRANDENBURG DIVISION

APRIL 1945

BRIDGE

RAILWAY

GERMAN ATTACK & DEFENCE POSITIONS

RUSSIAN ADVANCE & " "

Panzer Grenadier Division 'Brandenburg' in Defensive Battle Along the Neisse River, April 1945

By the Spring of 1945 the war in Europe was nearing its end and while the Allied troops on the Western front were driving through the heartland of Germany the Red Army, which had approached to within 60 kilometres of Berlin, was preparing the offensive which would capture the political and administrative centre of the Third Reich.

The foundations for the final Soviet drive to end the war had been laid between January and March when the winter offensive had paused, momentarily, to regroup before undertaking the last thrust. By mid-April Soviet Army Groups or Fronts, as they were sometimes called, were moving westwards once again and one of those Fronts, 1st Ukrainian, is the one with which this section deals. The battle line of that formation extended from Gross Gastrose in the north to the borders of Czechoslovakia in the south and before it lay a terrain heavily wooded and cut by several rivers of which the Neisse and the Spree were the most important.

As a pre-condition to its main role in the forthcoming offensive the Front was aiming to establish bridgeheads on the western bank of the Neisse river from which it would burst out, westwards, protecting the left flank of the great southern pincer arm swinging towards Berlin. This part of its role was to be carried out by five of the infantry armies and two of the tank armies in its order of battle. The 1st Ukrainian Front also had a secondary task, that of attacking along a line from Bautzen to Dresden for which it would field a further two armies. Collaborating in this lesser drive and helping to maintain the impetus would be a Guards Mechanised Corps and 1st Guards Cavalry Corps. The plan of 1st Ukrainian Front High Command was that the infantry would make the initial assault attacking behind a precisely regulated barrage of 2 hours and 25 minutes duration and covered by a smoke screen laid by aircraft. Once the river line had been forced the armour would be pushed through to thrust southwestwards towards Dresden and westwards to Leipzig.

Facing this huge Soviet build-up were the weak and understrength divisions of Army Group Centre which lay to the south of Berlin and directly opposite the 1st Ukrainian Front. Included in the order of battle of that Army Group was the crack *Grossdeutschland* Armoured Corps which had risen from an elite infantry guard regiment to Corps level and included among its subordinate formations the *Brandenburg*

Eastern Front, winter 1943-44. Panzer grenadiers passing a PzKw IV.

Panzer grenadiers, both armoured and motorised, of the Leibstandarte SS 'Adolf Hitler' *panzer division on the Eastern Front late in 1944.*

Waffen-SS panzer grenadiers regrouping after a local counter-attack. Eastern Front, winter 1944.

Division. It is about the *Jäger* (or Grenadiers) of that formation and of their battles against the 52nd Red Army and the 2nd Polish Army that this account deals.

The *Grossdeutschland* or *GD* Corps had reached the Neisse river in February 1945, after weeks of a fighting withdrawal from the Vistula river in Poland, and had been given a length of front which ran from Forst via Muskau to Sänitz. Among its neighbours were elements from 1st *Hermann Göring* Panzer Parachute Division and 20th Panzer Division. In the months which had elapsed since taking up position along the river the Corps had built defensive works and had resisted the pressure which the Red Army was beginning to exert again. This pressure was not equal along the whole length of the battle line and on some sectors of Army Group Centre there was little if any activity. At others, however, the vigorous patrolling by the 1st Ukrainian Front had enabled it to gain small footholds on the western bank of the Neisse river, particularly at Gross Sarchen and at Kobeln, against which the Germans had had to employ radio-controlled demolition tanks before the Soviet incursions could be eliminated.

During the first week of April *Brandenburg* Division was moved to the southern sector of the Corps front and took post from Wehrkirch to Steinbach. The Division committed both its *Jäger* (panzer grenadier) regiments to hold the front line while behind this the villages, towns and hamlets were put into a state of all round defence. Cellars of houses were converted into machine-gun positions; every high window became a sniper's nest and each tower an observation post. Experienced NCO's were sent out to recruit, train and lead young men of the Hitler Youth organisation in tank-busting teams.

By the afternoon of Sunday 15 April, it was clear that the Soviet offensive against Army Group Centre would begin on the following day. A small bridgehead which *Brandenburg* had on the eastern bank at Muskau was evacuated and throughout the day, while the rest of the front waited for the onslaught to begin, pioneers of the Red Army began attempts at bridging the Neisse which was, along parts of *Brandenburg* sector only 15 yards wide and in most places only 3 feet deep. Their first attempts were flung back or destroyed but during the afternoon they finally succeeded in throwing a few assault bridges over the river and of establishing bridgeheads, jumping off points for the imminent offensive.

Counter-attacks were launched but the Soviet perimeters were expanded, or were increased in number. In some places the Germans succeeded in driving the Red infantry back to the river bank and back across the Neisse, but at other places Russian footholds were gained and expanded in hand to hand fighting. By now the Soviets were too strong to be ejected and *Brandenburg* could only seal off the area and wait until next morning when, reinforced with reserves, it would counter-attack the lodgement areas. At about 23.00 hrs on Sunday 15 April, the Soviet bombardment which had persisted all day, died away for a short time. The firing of small arms diminished and in those quiet hours the men of *Brandenburg* Reserve Company came up and slipped into position in the slit trenches surrounding the Red perimeter, ready to begin the counter-attack at first light.

During the night both sides prepared themselves emotionally for the coming struggle. On the German side Hitler's Order of the Day exhorted his soldiers to 'defend the soil of the German homeland from the Asiatic hordes' while Soviet political commissars encouraged their men to look forward to 'smashing the Fascist beast in his lair'. While thus emotionally the two sides drew courage and confidence from their respective propaganda sources, on the material side the battle had already opened and artillery, machine-guns, mortars, and batteries of rocket launchers were being unleashed for that fight which both sides knew would be the last deciding battle.

At 05.00 hrs on a fine April morning the 1st Ukrainian Front erupted when hundreds of guns and thousands of mortars, after a few

A column of late-production SdKfz 251's in winter camouflage in December 1944.

A group of panzer grenadiers moving forward through deep snow in the Ardennes, 1944.

hours pause to re-ammunition, re-opened the barrage and broke the calm as their shells rained into the German lines. For 40 minutes the full fury of the barrage was poured upon all the positions. Then for a further hour it saturated the defenders on the western bank while under its hail Soviet infantry reached the eastern river bank and began to cross the assault bridges which had been constructed. Then the barrage lifted and walked into the German rear areas to prevent reinforcements from counter-attacking the fresh Russian penetrations. Under cover of this barrage and hidden in the smoke screen, which arcraft had laid and maintained throughout the duration of the barrage, the Soviet infantry of the second wave rose from the fields in which they had been laying and at 05.40 hrs advanced in columns to support the initial assault which was now about to begin.

In a fury of impatience men of 58th Guards Division did not wait their turn to cross the bridges but waded across the Neisse, holding their rifles and machine-guns above their heads. Guards Pioneers supported the wooden beams of one light bridge upon their shoulders to allow an assault detachment of 300 men to rush the German defences. Other infantry using boats, assault craft and even pieces of wood flung themselves across the narrow river; some even swam.

Quickly the Soviet groups consolidated on the west bank of the Neisse and on their move inland met the first of the panzer grenadier counter-attacks. The grenadier tactics were short, simple and effective: a heavy but brief mortar shell barrage followed by a controlled rush with maximum fire from machine-pistols and machine-guns and close assault weapons. The 2nd Regiment grenadiers closed with the Soviet enemy and drove him back to the river bank. But as fast as the Russians were driven back from one sector they flung more bridges across in another area, for all the approaches were flooded with khaki

Panzer grenadiers in a hastily-prepared defensive position early in 1945.

Tanks and armoured personnel carriers of a battle group in action.

uniformed men moving down to cross the river. The numbers they lost were enormous but their build up so rapid that at one point at which they had established a foothold their pioneers had, by 09.00 hrs constructed a heavy bridge across which the first vehicles, tanks and SP artillery were brought into action. With this support the Soviets began to enlarge the perimeter and the grenadiers in a fury of despair flung in counter-attack after counter-attack, trying to smash the Reds back into the Neisse river. Against one bridgehead into which the Soviets had crammed a battalion of men *Brandenburg* could field only one company and a platoon and even this small group was reduced by losses suffered in the continual mortar bombardments.

The sustained ferocity of the Soviet barrage destroyed the German front lines and as the Russian troops moved into the woods south east of Kahle Meile there was no sound of opposition from along the *Brandenburg* front. It seemed as if the entire German garrison had been destroyed in the fury of the guns and, indeed, most of 2nd Regiment's 1st battalion was rolled over as the Red advance pushed relentlessly forward to reach the railway line. The Soviet thrust, by accident or design, had struck along the boundary of 1st *Brandenburg* battalion and that of 1st battalion 1244th regiment. All communication with divisional headquarters had been destroyed by shell fire. The whole centre of the Division had been torn open and there grew the danger that the 1st regiment, as yet untouched by the assault, would be by-passed and isolated. Indeed the armoured personnel carrier battalion of that regiment had already been committed and the absence of news from the sector allotted to it indicated that it had probably been destroyed in the fighting.

Across the narrow river and into the perimeter poured a stream of Soviet tanks and then with a roar of movement the Red armour burst out of the confines of the lodgement area and flooded out in two mighty columns, the one heading north and the other westwards. Their intentions were plain: they intended to bypass, outflank and roll up 2nd Regiment's positions. Fighting desperately for time in which to establish a cohesive defence line the survivors of 1st battalion flung in attack after attack but the armoured might of the Soviets crushed and overran those remnants. Isolated groups heading westward from the crumbling front were overtaken by the Red armour or were intercepted by their patrols and captured. Other groups went to ground in shell holes and in bomb craters allowing the waves of Soviet infantry and armour to sweep over them planning to escape through the lines and to rejoin their comrades.

Other *Brandenburg* groups, unheeded by the tanks which were roaring through the gap where once 1st battalion had held post, fired into the flanks of the Soviet assault as it passed them wreaking damage out of all proportion to their numbers until the Russian second wave armour went in to engage the pockets of resistance and destroyed them one by one. In the rear area of 1st battalion's sector a desperate race against time was being fought. Cooks, drivers, batmen and other non-combatant soldiers were organised into defensive positions so as to form a line along the railway against which the Soviet drive might be halted for a while until a firmer line had been established farther to the west. This forlorn hope of grenadiers stood its ground and opened fire—a thin line of men issued with small arms to resist a sea of armour. The unequal struggle did not last long and the T-34's and JS heavy tanks crushed into the ground the bodies of 1st battalion's remnants. Other lines were formed from men hastily assembled and sent in to hold the Red advance; each succeeding line fought and died under the tank tracks. Division took the only choice left to it. It would withdraw from the battle zone faster than the Soviets could pursue it and with short breathing space thus gained would form a cohesive line and an effective block to the Soviet advance, which had by now developed along the whole *Brandenburg* front. Each of its subordinate units was embattled.

Assault pioneers of the Division fighting as grenadiers stood their ground when they came under attack in the wooded area around Geheege. In that area the Soviet soldiers were striking forward in a joint armoured and infantry column from Biehain towards the tactically important hill, Point 188. Once again non-combatant personnel were put into the line, for Hill 188 had been selected by divisional headquarters as the first point at which the Red break through would be temporarily halted. There were no trained infantrymen or grenadiers to hold the line and the drivers, cooks and other rear echelon personnel prepared to face the Russian storm while in the thick forests the Pioneer/grenadiers played a deadly game with the Soviet tanks, killing them in close quarter fighting. Such was the determined resistance around Geheege that the Soviet thrust was deflected and changed direction towards Ober-Wehrkirch whose garrison also included men from the Pioneer battalion. At Ober-Wehrkirch there was a large estate and park within which three 8.8 cm Flak guns were positioned, the last reserve of an artillery battalion whose batteries were in the line supporting the grenadier regiments. The Pioneer/grenadiers and the flak gunners prepared themselves for the imminent battle; already the castle was under artillery fire.

The divisional commander ordered a counter-attack by one battalion of 2nd regiment, to thrust through to Kaltwasser to support other battalions which had so far held back the Soviet assaults. But before the relieving attack could reach the isolated units from out of the surrounding woods poured wave after wave of Red armour and infantry which then deployed and swept down in attack. Anti-tank guns opened up at the armoured flood and tank after tank was crippled or destroyed. But however many vehicles were hit from over the crest of the hill poured new waves and they roared towards Kaltwasser, smashing down the *Brandenburg* opposition outside the town with their heavy calibre tank guns. In the narrow streets the Grenadiers held the advantage and the number of T-34's destroyed rose as they were killed at point-blank range with *Panzerfaust* rockets, but against such continual reinforcing there could only be one end and the defenders were forced out of the town. They moved off to the divisional concentration area and as the weary groups of men rested, hidden in the forest along a railway line, there passed before their eyes the incredible sight of packed columns of Red infantry, striding out as if on a route march, not deployed for battle, heading for the fighting now far to the west.

The only clear picture which could be gained was that the Soviets

A typical panzer grenadier section leader (left) and an assault gun battery commander of the 'Grossdeutschland' division (right). Note the distinguishing 'GD' insignia on his shoulder straps.

were everywhere. *Brandenburg* patrols north of Wehrkirch on the Rothenburg—Uhsmannsdorf road reported that Soviet tank columns, masses of horse drawn carts and guns had bypassed Wehrkirch and were thrusting down from Nieder Wehrkirch using the railway line as the axis of advance.

The first massive Soviet assault had ruptured the *Brandenburg* line and had destroyed the cohesion of 2nd Regiment, transmuting it from a single force into groups of desperate men holding out and fighting in the villages and hamlets which they had fortified. Detachments of various sizes were in the Geheege estate, in Wehrkirch and in the surrounding villages of Ober- and Nieder Wehrkirch. In the woods groups of grenadiers separated from their parent formations slipped past Russian posts to regain their battalions and to continue the fight.

The isolated groups of German defenders were under repeated and furious assault. The Pioneer/grenadiers swung a skirmishing line into the forests to the west of Geheege and then fought their way towards Nieder Wehrkirch. The pioneer assault then went in against the houses of the town occupied by the Red Army and in the fury of the attack the Soviets were driven from the buildings in complete confusion. In the Wehrkirch estate park the small garrison loopholed the massive stone walls which surrounded the estate. Through these the 8.8 cm Flak guns brought the Soviet tanks under fire but although they destroyed many of them the waves of T-34's roared nearer and

A group of panzer grenadiers huddled behind the turret of an PzKw IV going into action.

nearer. Then it was the time for individual grenadiers and tank-busting teams armed with *Panzerfausts* and explosive charges to take on the steel giants. With the dexterity of long years of combat, with the precision of *banderillos* and all through the long hot afternoon the grenadiers stalked the tanks, picking them off even though each was accompanied by groups of Red infantry. To support their attacking troops the Soviets brought up reinforcements in open lorries and these too were attacked and destroyed. The fierceness of the German defence and the aggressiveness of the tank-destroyer teams forced the Soviets to withdraw and they moved back to the houses in Wehrkirch in which they waited for reinforcements to arrive before they would move out against the *Brandenburg* troops.

Then came a welcome addition to the strength of the small garrison: more 8.8 cm Flak guns arrived and were immediately put into action to protect the flanks. Reinforcements of grenadiers came in and added to the numbers and then even more guns so that at last a perimeter with all round defence could be established. By late evening men from a Company of engineers had arrived within the walls and with these new additions the garrison commander felt himself sufficiently strong to make limited assaults against the Soviet troops in Wehrkirch. The assault groups went in fighting their way from house to house, mouseholing from room to room. In the gathering darkness of the late spring night there was little time for challenge and response. It was a matter of flinging open a door, putting in a burst of sub-machine-gun fire and a handgrenade or two and then on to the next room, or else to burst from the house round a corner where a Russian post might be waiting. At some points the Red defenders fought hand to hand with knife and bayonet and then it was the vicious blows from entrenching tools and gun butts which beat down the opposition. By 22.00 hrs much of Wehrkirch had been recaptured, but the fighting had reduced the numbers of grenadiers and had exhausted the survivors. The counter-attack could win no more ground that night.

While bitter fighting had been the lot of 2nd Regiment its sister formation, occupying positions between Rothenburg and Steinbach,

A 'Marder' tank destroyer armed with a 7.5 cm Pak on PzKw II chassis of the 'Hermann Göring' division.

had not initially been under heavy pressure. Then during the early afternoon the situation changed and assault aircraft of the Red Air Force swept low over the regimental positions bombing and machine-gunning to soften up the defences. Under cover of these assaults waves of tanks rumbled forward and the situation immediately became fluid. There were reports received of Soviet tanks in Spree while other news of fire upon 2nd battalion, in position near Bleichenau, indicated that Soviet infantry had infiltrated through or around the positions and that the whole 1st Regiment was, in all probability, surrounded. The German defences in the area seemed to have been completely destroyed, for grenadier observers south of Rothenburg saw long columns of Red infantry and tanks moving forward unopposed by infantry nor under fire from German artillery.

The situation for the *Brandenburg* Division on the evening of 16 April was chaotic. The Soviet thrust had torn open its front on a width of 8 kms and Russian tank spearheads were reported to have formed a salient extending to a depth of 15 kms west of the Neisse river. Lacking communication with his divisional headquarters and acting upon his own initiative the commander of 1st Regiment swung his unit southwards, not so much in the hope of forming a new defensive line as of moving against the salient which held the Soviet forces, of cutting of their spearhead units and of destroying them piecemeal.

While his regiment was striking southwards in other divisional sectors frantic efforts were made to sort out the jumble of units and to tidy the battle line. The difficulties of the situation were increased as there was not only no contact between the battalions and their divisional headquarters, but also that individual battalions were out of touch with each other. The divisional front, if such it could be termed, was held by the main of 2nd Regiment holding position in and around Kodersdorf and Mückenhain, while the main of 1st regiment was in the woods to the east of Hähnichen. A third, smaller, group made up of elements from the artillery regiment, the anti-aircraft battalion and the Pioneer/grenadiers held positions in and around the Wehrkirch area.

In the early morning of 17 April the fighting which had rumbled in

125

low key all night burst once again into full fury and once again the main weight of the Soviet pressure fell upon the remnants of 2nd Regiment's 1st battalion at Kodersdorf. The dreadfully reduced companies holding hamlets and houses were faced with two bitter alternatives: either to stand and die, or to withdraw to Ullersdorf where a skirmishing line had been set up. The 1st battalion staged a fighting retreat back to Ullersdorf and the Red assault then swung into the flank of 3rd battalion forcing it to fall back.

But in Wehrkirch the unyielding garrison, supported by artillery, was fighting gallantly as it battled for its life. The first of a series of Red tank assaults went in at 03.00 hrs and in the garish light of flares and signal rockets the gunners destroyed more than 40 Soviet armoured fighting vehicles. The battle was fought at all ranges. The 8.8 cm Flak guns picked off the tanks at long distances; the lighter anti-tank artillery broke up the assaults at medium range and, where the weight of the attack swamped the gun line, then the tank-destroyer comman- dos went out and smashed back the Russian assaults.

At 09.00 hrs the Soviet artillery laid down a heavy barrage of such fury and duration that it was feared that the Wehrkirch garrison would be destroyed by gunfire. It was isolated and had fulfilled its purpose; the initial impetus of the Red advance had been slowed. There was nothing to be gained from further sacrifices. Wehrkirch was evacuated and moving by bounds, covering each other by fire and movement, the small parties of the German defenders withdrew through a countryside swarming with Soviet soldiers.

Division fell back to a new line running from Niesky, via Neuhof to Rietschen, but barely had the regiments taken up their positions than they were under attack from a flood of tanks forming the Red spearhead. Desperate times call for desperate measures and calling upon every effort the grenadiers flung back the Red armoured flood. In the short space that elapsed between the resumption of the Soviet attack the *Brandenburg* regiments sent out patrols to dominate the forward zone and to establish the strength of the Red build up.

A sudden Soviet thrust against Niesky sent the grenadier outpost line around that town back and pressure built up against each defended point along the *Brandenburg* sector. Batteries of 8.8 cm Flak guns guarded the road to Rietschen and supported the defence of the villages in the area within which the grenadiers had taken up defensive positions. Kodersdorf, Hähnichen and Ullersdorf formed the corner stones of the defensive line.

However little resistance the *Brandenburg* had been able to put up against the Soviet drive it had, together with other factors, been sufficient to cause the Soviet Command to regroup it forces. The 52nd Red Army, Swierczewski's 2nd Polish Army and the Guards Divisions were quickly reorganised and put back into the assault. The renewed drive quickly captured the town of Weisswasser, which had formed a pillar of the right flank defences and allowed the Soviet troops to flood forward into and then past the town of Spree. The grenadiers who had held the place then escaped to strengthen the defences at Hähnichen. The pace of the Russian advance accelerated, and concurrently with the arrival of the former garrison of Spree the first signs of an impending Red assault were observed. Soviet infantry had slipped quickly through the woods around Hähnichen and had reached a height dominating the town to the east. Then they emerged from the cover of the trees and flooded down the wooden slopes, pouring in a brown flood across the meadows towards the little market town. Quickly the SP guns, which formed the heavy weapons of the garrison, moved out to engage the infantry and checked them. The Soviets bypassed the town swinging left and right of the place and having then surrounded it began an attack from both an easterly and westerly direction. While the German garrison was thus busily engaged the Soviet Command pushed other columns on towards Rietschen and thrust a new spearhead southwestwards from Weisswasser, bringing with it a renewal of the threat that both 1st regiment and the Pioneer battalion would be cut off. Still out of contact with divisional headquarters the regiment placed itself, temporarily, under the command of 615 Special Division.

The Soviet High Command did not intend to be held up by Niesky and they flung their armoured spearheads past the town. Dawn on 18

Transported close to the battle area, a group of panzer grenadiers of the 'Grossdeutschland' division are given last-minute instructions. This SdKfz 251 is temporarily used as a command vehicle.

Command vehicles and a tank of the 'Grossdeutschland' division. The 'white steel helmet' symbol was the divisional insignia.

April saw their armoured force heading in a two column drive, one for the main Dresden trunk road while the other thrust for Bautzen. Behind the tank point units came the mass of the Red Army forcing back the *Brandenburg* line. Quitzendorf and See were given up and the flak batteries halting to regroup at Gross Radisch saw from the high ground on which they were positioned the ground before them covered with extended lines or close packed columns of the Russian main body moving as irresistably as a brown flood, occupying the abandoned towns and villages or mopping up those pockets of grenadiers which, although surrounded, had still carried on the fight. Some small Grenadier garrisons, none larger than thirty men, did not wait to the submerged in the tide of the Soviet advance but struck through the surrounding masses of the Red Army to regain the German lines.

Such had been the speed of the Soviet advance that between the Neisse and the town of Bautzen the only organised resistance was being offered in Niesky and a few other places, standing like rocks in the onsweeping flood. The time was fast approaching when these troops, like those in smaller villages and hamlets would have to escape or go under, but one thing alone tied them to these indefensible outposts. Hitler's order had been explicit: stand fast and do not surrender one foot of German soil. This inflexible command condemned the German defenders to die without being able to influence the Soviet advance in any way. The *Grossdeutschland* Corps headquarters in Spreefurth was

Heavy artillery of the 'Grossdeutschland' division being rail-transported to another sector of the Eastern Front.

A Company commander observing the battlefield from an SdKfz 251 of the 'Grossdeutschland' division.

forbidden to leave the town on Hitler's direct order, even though Soviet columns had, in fact, outflanked the town to the north-west. The whole Corps front had fragmented into a series of small groups attempting to halt the Red advance, but there were too many spearheads to be held back and Soviet tank groups were reported from a number of places behind what was considered to be the German Front.

In Boxberg a slight breathing space was gained by the tenacity of the Pioneer/grenadier defence. The Soviet tanks had reached the town but had not seized it, and having regrouped were preparing to carry forward their advance when the last SP guns of the *GD* armoured artillery brigade and part of the Pioneer battalion struck them. Both these units had fought their way out of encirclement and had barely had time to rest and re-organise themselves before the Soviet tank waves had swept down upon them. From the slopes of the Boxberg the *GD* self-propelled artillery bombarded the T-34's at long range, picking them off as they roared toward the base of the hill and causing them to deploy before coming on again. The halted tanks then came under the close assault of the pioneers who with rockets and explosive charges threw confusion into the Red squadrons, forcing them into the open country where they again came under fire from the SP guns.

Other Pioneers in Niesky still held out against the Russian effort that was overwhelming both in power and in the numbers involved. Thunderous barrages fell upon the houses of the small town and infantry assaults succeeded each other at less than hourly intervals.

One squadron of Red tanks which broke through a barricade was destroyed with 'Molotov cocktails' and hollow explosive charges. The burning hulks then formed a stonger barricade than that which they had pierced. But the German troops were not content merely to fight off the Soviet assaults. They flung in their own counter-attacks, often to recapture houses with particularly good fields of fire, oft-times to ease the pressure and at other times to establish their superiority over the Soviet troops opposite them. The defence stood firm realising that so long as the ammunition, food and water held out they could deny this crossroads town to the Soviets. A Soviet demand for the surrender of the town was refused; their offers of good treatment turned down. The Pioneer/grenadiers fought on using a tactic which had proved itself to be the most effective in urban conditions. As the Soviet infantry swept through the streets in attack the grenadiers held their fire until at 40 metres the enemy was met and struck by a hail of *Panzerfaust* anti-tank rockets whose explosions tore away the leading waves. Then the fast-firing MG 42's and sub-machine-guns took advantage of the confusion. The Soviet troops fell in hundreds in one gallant but vain attempt after the other. But the surprise tactics were not restricted only to the grenadiers. Russian counter tactics were to suddenly fire a strong mortar barrage immediately ahead of their own men, catching the German troops as they emerged to engage the attacking Reds.

Panzer grenadiers of a mortar section await orders to advance.

Panzer grenadiers in an SdKfz 250 armed with a 3.7 cm anti-tank gun.

West of Kodersdorf and Ullersdorf the 2nd *Brandenburg* Regiment found touch with elements from 20th Panzer Division and thus formed an unbroken line in that sector. Slowly the German defence east of Spreefurth was setting firm, and to facilitate this the *Brandenburg* units placed themselves under the command of the next major formation as 1st Regiment had already done. The situation was, however, still very fluid in other parts of the front and symptomatic of that state was the situation which occurred during the night of 20 April. Part of 1st regiment moving through the Muskau forest to reach the safety of the Boxberg and Spreefurth, could not be told by wireless or telephone that the Russians had already reached as far as those places. But when they became aware of the situation the grenadiers fell upon the backs of the Soviet troops, crushed them against the narrow river Schöps which flows through Boxberg town and forced those who had escaped the onslaught to flee into the surrounding woods. Grenadier patrols went out to establish the situation around Spreefurth, and 1st

Regiment was ordered to recapture the town of Klitten and then to go on and capture other villages in order that a line could be formed.

For now the time had come when the first Soviet thrusts were slowing down and the opportunity was presented not only to concentrate the grenadier units but also strike against the Red spearheads and to halt their drive. Accordingly, those formations which were able swung into the assault while those, like the Pioneer/grenadiers at Niesky, who had no chance to offensive action, realised they they were bastions of a possible future strong defence line and held out determinedly against the assaults of the enemy.

The concentration of 1st Regiment and its supporting battalion of artillery for the forthcoming attack upon Klitten was delayed. The lack of communication together with the unclear situation regarding the location of the Soviet troops and, not least, the roads choked with refugees fleeing from the bombardments and from the fear of Russian reprisals, so upset the timetable that it was not until evening that the final preparations had been completed. At last light the assault opened; the grenadiers thrust forward, fought a hard, bitter little battle, consolidated in the town which they had captured, and prepared to resume the drive during the following morning. Their next objectives were Radisch, Altmarkt and Ullersdorf, all of which had recently fallen into Soviet hands. It was planned to retake these in a pincer operation. The 1st Regiment would strike southwards to meet an upward thrust by 2nd Regiment and elements from 20th Panzer Division.

In the morning of 20 April, detachments from 2nd Regiment, supported by tanks, struck at Ullersdorf. The Red garrison included Poles and communists from the Free German Committee, and so fierce was the resistance to the grenadiers that the town was burned out and destroyed in the fighting. Despite this defence Ullersdorf was captured but Jankendorf, 2nd Regiment's next objective, could not be taken. The regiment had fought itself to a standstill.

The Pioneer/grenadiers surrounded in Niesky summoned up the last reserves of strength to drive back the Red assaults. Slightly wounded grenadiers, determined that their absence should not weaken the defence, insisted upon returning to the front line once their wounds had been dressed. Against such a spirit the Red assaults were frustrated and fighting died down during the morning, for the Russian troops too had been exhausted by their fruitless assaults. The Soviet command sent reinforcements and in their haste to commit these fresh troops to battle had them brought forward in soft-skinned lorries and to within gun range of an SP. The gunners engaged their targets over open sights and blew the lorries apart in quick succession. They then engaged the infantry who had escaped this destruction and who had been formed up on the open road and then set marching into battle in column and without having been deployed in artillery formation. Under the accurate barrage the battalions were smashed and the reinforcements brought up to lead the new series of attacks were destroyed before they could be brought to battle.

As neither armour nor infantry had been able to take the town the Soviet Command sent the Cossack cavalry in during the late morning. These, too, were cut down in swathes. Once again the tactic which had proved itself against the infantry was applied and found suitable against cavalry. *Panzerfausts* fired at close range and followed by intense machine-gun and sub-machine-gun fire destroyed the Cossack assaults. Red infantry was sent in again storming forward over the bodies of the fallen from other and equally unsuccessful charges. Every hour their attacks were repeated for now the only remaining tactic was attrition, with assaults coming in from every direction but always precisely timed. This rigidity was a defect for it allowed the last three SP guns to be switched from one danger point to another and they, the mobile artillery defence of Niesky, by well-aimed fire from concealed positions held and flung back the Soviet drive.

It was clear that the town must eventually fall to the unrelenting pressure and those few remaining civilians in the town asked to know when *Brandenburg* intended to evacuate. The situation had become hopeless. There were no dressings for the wounded, and sheets and other household linen had had to be taken. Casualties were mounting and the numbers of men manning the line were insufficient to hold the perimeter. An escape plan was worked out. During the night the break-out would occur. Behind an advance guard would come a caravan of about 200 refugees carried on broken down lorries towed by the SP guns. The preparations were completed, the wounded made as comfortable as possible for the difficult journey which lay ahead of them and then, before the town was evacuated, the *Brandenburg* dead were buried with as much ceremony as it was possible to give them, for the ground in which they would be interred would on the morrow be occupied by an alien enemy.

Reconnaissance patrols went out probing the encircling Red ring until a weak spot was found through which at 02.00 hrs of 21 April the break out was made. The column passed through a series of narrow country roads until it reached the Niesky by-pass and entered the main Soviet-held area. There was no sound as they passed through the darkened countryside; no challenge, no sudden burst of fire to indicate that their escape had been detected. Back in Niesky a rearguard went round the perimeter, occasionally firing a burst from a machine-gun to convince the Soviets that the garrison was still holding out. Then came the time when the rearguard itself had to leave to join the main body of the escape column. At a crossroads there was a sudden challenge and a burst of fire but by indicating their position the Red sentries had marked themselves for death. Quickly a grenadier group swung into action holding the attention of the Soviet troops to the front while a second group outflanked the sentries. There was a short burst from sub-machine-guns; a detonation of hand grenades and it was over. The road ahead was clear.

A second alarming incident happened just before dawn when the column was pursued by a Soviet motorised detachment. But this Red unit was not aware that the slow moving column was a German one and rapidly overhauled it, moving at speed towards the sound of the guns. The grenadiers and their refugees turned southwards through the Russian artillery belt and then reached the German outpost line at Särchen shortly after dawn.

Back at Ullersdorf the offensive to cut off the Red spearhead had begun with an attack by the southern pincer made up of 1st battalion of the 2nd Regiment. The grenadiers supported by panzers seized the

Panzer grenadiers in the defence of the Reich: men of a battle-group in the forests of East Prussia awaiting a Soviet attack.

heights dominating the northern edge of town but their thrust into the southern part of Ullersdorf was, at first, held by a determined Red defence. Then a foothold was gained—a few houses—and from this slight lodgement the grenadiers fought their way, room to room, from house to house, from street to street gaining ground all the time. But even as they advanced the losses which they were suffering reduced their drive until by nightfall only a few of the original force were still alive and unwounded. The assault faltered and halted for lack of manpower. Then came the Soviet counter-attacks, driving the gre-

An armoured division in battle, photographed, by a panzer grenadier.

nadiers from the positions which they had won until they held only a small perimeter along the southern edge of town.

The northern pincer assault had had better luck and 1st Regiment's 2nd battalion, striking out of Klitten, carried out a frontal assault under the support of a pair of SP guns. The Soviet defenders of Zimpel, the first village on the route to the final objective, put up a most determined resistance which involved the grenadiers in house to house fighting. Then Soviet tanks appeared on the scene and these were fought at close quarters by the *Brandenburg* grenadiers. The SP commander realised that the Soviets intended to feed the garrison of Zimpel with reinforcements, and flung out a wide encircling move to cut off this flow of help. Starved of support Zimpel fell and the grenadiers thrust through the village with its few streets littered with the destroyed and burning T-34's which had tried in vain to halt the German advance. Tauer was the next objective, and this was taken by nightfall.

The Pioneer/grenadiers, now refreshed by a few hours of rest, had no intention of being left out of the battle and supported 1st regiment by capturing a succession of villages and carrying the drive forward through the woods at Dauban to cut the Bautzen road, the main artery along which the Soviet spearhead was being nourished. By swift and determined assault the Reds in Dauban were surrounded and destroyed, and with the fall of that place other Soviet positions were open to attack and fell, one after the other. The *Brandenburg* assault gained more ground.

The 1st Regiment's 2nd battalion, in a night march, struck towards the strongly held town of Förstgen intending to assault it on the morning of the next day, The difficulties of terrain made the operation a difficult one, for the town lay behind a natural barrier made up of a chain of small lakes connected by thick woods. A holding group from the battalion was left south of Tauer while the main went through the woods before opening its assault. The 2nd battalion was also to take part in the operation and was to strike the town from the north-west and under a barrage fired by SP artillery. In the woods the battalion divided; the grenadiers to reach their start line and the SPs to thrust round the outside of the town and to strike it from the south east. At 14.30 hrs the German barrage opened, the grenadiers struck down the hill supported by a line of 2 cm Flak and covered by the SP barrage. The pace of the advance brought them storming into the town where they destroyed the Soviet garrison. Soviet tanks were sent in to restore the situation, but these the grenadiers destroyed in close-combat fighting. Over 50 tanks, more than a hundred vehicles and other booty fell into German hands. The Red infantry withdrew in a confusion which manifested itself later during the attack which the Red regiments made upon the Pioneer/grenadiers, during the afternoon of 22 April.

Against the Pioneers the Soviets sent in counter-attacks of massed infantry riding on a battle wedge of tanks. The attacks went into recapture a crossroads, a key position which they had lost in the early stages of the *Brandenburg* penetration. Accurate and heavy machine-gun and mortar fire forced the Reds to leave the tanks on which they had been riding and the infantry continued to advance on foot threatening the thin *Brandenburg* line with extinction. Then a single

Panther tank rolled forward, took up an enfilade position and from cover of a house into which it had been driven, began to destroy the armoured wedge. The tactic was an old one: kill the last tank, then the second from last and continue along the line. Tank after tank blew up, slewed round crippled or began to burn, and the Red infantry seeing their support destroyed, began to waver, then to halt and finally to withdraw. As they moved back the Pioneer/grenadiers rose from their fox holes and stood on the parapets, the better to pour volley after volley into the backs of their retreating enemies. A rout ensued.

The unexpectedly strong resistance offered to the Soviets by the handful of German grenadier regiments and battalions had turned the Red tide, and the spearhead troops were flooding back eastwards to regain touch with the main body of the advance. The tenacious *Brandenburg* defence had also achieved a strategic result for the Soviet plan to thrust towards Dresden could not succeed and had been deflected north-eastwards. Indeed, the main thrust of 1st Ukrainian Front had turned almost due north to bolster the pincer operation around Berlin and, into the gap which had been created by this swing, the Soviets put in Guards and other elite troops to add weight to the crushing attack against the *Brandenburgers*.

During the early hours of 23 April, the Pioneer/grenadiers made contact with patrols from 1st Regiment and the two units then combined and struck southwards towards the main highway. Their drive took them across the Red axis of advance and was carried out without severe opposition being encountered. In the thrust the German attack captured Graudnitz from the Russian garrison. The *GD* Corps then ordered Division to regroup for an attack upon the town of Weissenburg through which Soviet forces, cut off by the *Brandenburg* pincer operation, were seeking to escape.

From the hills surrounding the town German observers noted that the streets were choked with vehicles and that traffic jams had brought to a halt the Red attempts to withdraw from the *Brandenburg* pincers. Quickly the SP artillery rolled into position and heavy howitzers were brought into line. Under a short sharp barrage the grenadier battalions of 1st Regiment poured over the start line, raced down the Weissenberg and struck the town from the northwest. Then the 2nd Regiment flung a pincer round the town to prevent the enemy from escaping southwards or southeastwards. Under the fury of the bombardment and the impact of a mortar barrage, a rain of *Panzerfausts* and a hail of machine-gun bullets a wild panic ensued, and the Soviets tried to force a way through the blocking positions held by 2nd Regiment. Tactically, they could not have chosen a worse area in which to carry out such an attempt. The ground to the southeast of the town was a flat plain with no folds in which to hide, nor woods in which to lie concealed. The grenadier line pretended to weaken so as to entice the Reds into the killing ground; and the plan succeeded. The Soviet forces were drawn into a salient. Within a short space of time the whole south-east plain was covered as the Russians drove across the ground in lorries, in horse

A group of panzer grenadiers in defensive positions early in 1945. Two NSU 'Kettenkrad' tracked motorcycle carriers/tractors in the background.

A panzer grenadier company advancing cross-country in 1943—the forerunners of armoured mechanised assault infantry of today.

drawn carts, in orderly columns of infantry, galloping squadrons of horsemen and wild mobs of other soldiers whom panic had affected. The crash of the first German salvo brought chaos and confusion. Lorries and carts collided, riderless horses raced across the fields and the broken columns of foot soldiers roamed about in disorder. The units leading the break out halted in the fierce fire but the pressure of those behind them forced the advance to continue. And then the troops in the front fell in swathes as the machine-guns, barrels red hot from use, shot them down. Still the pressure from the rear was maintained and the panic-sticken retreat poured over the dead and dying and flooded as a mob towards the *Brandenburg* lines. The detonations from exploding shells could no longer by identified separately, they were part of a continuous roar of sound through which came, thinly, the screams of the wounded. Vast clouds of black smoke covered the sky as the lorries, carts and tanks were bombarded into flame but despite this sable smoke screen the *Brandenburg* grenadiers saw their enemy flee in disorder. To complete the rout the grenadiers, their spirits uplifted with this victory after so many days and weeks of despair, dashed into the attack, carrying out the most final of all infantry operations, a bayonet charge. The human prisoners numbered hundreds and the lorries taken exceeded one thousand. A whole Soviet division had been destroyed.

But the loss of one division to a force whose army enjoyed a 20 to 1 superiority in infantry was of slight concern to STAVKA. Of greater significance and danger to the *Grossdeutschland* Corps was the fact that Bautzen had fallen into the hands of the Soviets and those elements of Corps still fighting to the east of that place were in imminent danger of being destroyed. Army Group Centre ordered that every effort to made to recapture the town, and by the night of 25/26 April the 2nd *Brandenburg* Regiment had reached the divisional concentration area. The Pioneer/grenadiers and the SP artillery were deployed north of the Bautzen—Dresden road.

This was to be a major amputation of the Red thrust. *Brandenburg* together with 20th and 21st Panzer Divisions formed the left wing which was to strike northwards. The right wing of *Brandenburg* was made up of 2nd Regiment with the Pioneer/grenadiers forming the left wing and behind them the main of 1st Regiment. At zero hour the advance began and in a smooth, flowing assault territory lost during the fighting of the previous few days was quickly recaptured by 2nd Regiment. Against the Pioneer/grenadiers, however, the Red opposition was almost suicidal in its intensity. The Poles of the 2nd Army who held the ground conducted themselves with traditional Polish tenacity but their efforts at defence were frustrated by the shortcomings of their own artillery and armour. The *Brandenburg* SP artillery blew the T-34's apart with little trouble. Then the Pioneers brought in a weapon which they had themselves developed—aircraft cannon fitted on armoured personnel carriers. The very high rate of fire of these weapons wrought havoc among the Polish infantry and more than 600 badly shaken prisoners were taken.

The inevitable Red counter-attacks came in against 2nd Regiment: Soviet tanks roaming down to take the grenadiers in flank, but the capture of the village of Loga by the Pioneer/grenadiers had turned the Soviet flank and it was they who were stormed and who broke. More Red armour was put in against the Pioneer/grenadiers and under this new pressure the German advance halted. To bring the advance forward again the 1st Regiment moved through the Pioneer/grenadiers and struck at Neschwitz. This was a heavily defended key point in the Soviet defences for it was the jumping off point for the resumption of their delayed advance southwestwards. Deeply aware of the importance of Neschwitz to the Soviets, the *Brandenburg* struck hard and repeated blows to seize it but came up against a steel defence. The village changed hands several times, neither side having the strength to hold it, and both sides being determined not to let it pass into the hands of the enemy.

Soviet pressure built up against all the incursions of the *Brandenburgers*. The 2nd Regiment was involved in bitter fighting against the counter-attacks which were being made upon it and the Pioneer/grenadiers failed to capture Casslau with their first attack. The town was defended by a Guards Armoured Brigade which had been ordered to hold it to the last man and was determined to carry out that order. But the Pioneer/grenadiers were not to be gainsaid and flung in a second attack at 22.00 hrs which ejected the Red Guards from houses on the outskirts of the town. A third attack went in and gained a few more houses. Then isolated groups of men and tanks from 20th Panzer Division came in to support the drive and with this assistance, as well as support from a battalion of 1244th regiment whose men suffered from stomach ulcers, Casslau was finally captured. During the last fifteen minutes of the battle to destroy the Red troops no fewer than fifteen Soviet tanks were destroyed, one for every minute of the final phase.

The victories which had been gained were to be short lived however. The STAVKA flung in every man in furious assaults. In Neschwitz Soviet counter-attacks broke into the northern sector of that town and began to expand the extent of their lodgement area. In Casslau the Pioneer/grenadiers strengthened their positions, but despite this all was lost in a Red counter-attack launched with mass armour and supported by low flying armoured assault aircraft. The town had to be given up and the Pioneers withdrew to the edge of the woods outside the place. Even there they were harried and attacked by Soviet tanks which drove them back into the forests. Battalion headquarters organised counter-attacks to win back the town but each and every Pioneer/grenadier assault was destroyed by the Red armour. The whole of the *Brandenburg* front was under the most severe pressure and plans which Corps had formed to be undertaken on 29 April, were scrapped, for information had been received that the Division was to be relieved from the Bautzen area and put into action in the Dresden—Meissen sector. During the night the change over took place and the remaining *Brandenburg* grenadiers marched away from the Neisse line for a few days rest. They were to see battle again but this account of their actions along the Neisse river ends here.

The war had entered upon its closing stages. Only one day after the *Brandenburg* left the Neisse line, Adolf Hitler, the German Supreme Commander, committed suicide in Berlin and seven days after that event the unconditional surrender of the German Armed Forces ended the war in Europe. 'Grossdeutschland' as a military formation and *Grossdeutschland* as a political state had both ceased to exist.

Unit Histories

The following are the short histories of armoured formations, from Panzer Armies down to Panzer Grenadier Divisions, which included panzer grenadiers within their order of battle. It should be noted that armoured and motorised infantry divisions could be employed in non panzer-designated commands.

Motorised Infantry Divisions
(Retitled Panzer Grenadier in March 1943)

2nd Infantry Division (motorised)
Formed in 1937, it fought in Poland and the West, 1940. In December 1940 it was reorganised into 12th Panzer Division.

3rd Infantry Division (motorised)
Formed in October 1940, from 3rd Infantry Division, it fought in the East from June 1941 until it was destroyed at Stalingrad in January 1943. In March 1943 it was reformed from 386th Infantry Division (motorised), and in July moved to the South-West. From September 1944 it was in the West.

5th Light (Africa) Division
Formed in January 1941 before being moved to North Africa. In July 1941 it was reformed into 21st Panzer Division.

10th Infantry Division (motorised)
Formed in October 1940 from 10th Infantry Division, it served in the East from June 1941 until the end. By March 1944 it had been so badly mauled that it was combined with 273rd Reserve Panzer Division, but still retained its title.

13th Infantry Division (motorised)
Formed in 1937, it fought in Poland and in the West, 1940, and was reorganized into 13th Panzer Division in October of that year.

14th Infantry Division (motorised)
Formed in October 1940 from 14th Infantry Division, and fought in the Soviet Union from June 1941. In the summer of 1943 it was reorganised back again into an ordinary infantry division, the 14th.

15th Panzergrenadier Division
Formed in May 1943 from the remnants of 15th Panzer Division which had escaped from Tunisia. It fought in Italy until September 1944, when it moved to the Western Front.

16th Infantry Division (motorised)
Formed in September 1940 from parts of 16th Infantry Division. In April 1941 it took part in the Balkan campaign. On the Eastern Front from June 1941 until March 1944, when its remnants were organised within 116th Panzer Division.

18th Infantry Division (motorised)
Formed in October 1940 from 18th Infantry Division, and fought in the East from June 1941. In July 1944 it was destroyed on the Central Front, but was reformed and continued the fight on the Eastern Front from December until February 1945, when it was again decimated.

20th Infantry Division (motorised)
Formed in 1937, and fought in Poland, the West and in the East from June 1941.

25th Infantry Division (motorised)
Formed in October 1940 from 25th Infantry Division, and fought in the East from June 1941 until destroyed in July 1944 on the Central Front. Reformed in December 1944, it was deployed again on the Eastern Front from February 1945.

29th Infantry Division (motorised)
Formed in 1937, and fought in Poland, the West and in the East from June 1941 until destroyed at Stalingrad in January 1943. In March 1943 it was reformed from 345th Infantry Division and was employed in the South-West from July 1943 onwards.

36th Infantry Division (motorised)
Formed in October 1940 from 36th Infantry Division, and fought in the East from June 1941 until the summer of 1943, when it was reorganised back into an ordinary infantry division, the 36th.

60th Infantry Division (motorised)
Formed in October 1940 from 60th Infantry Division. It fought in the Balkan campaign in April 1941 and in the East from June 1941 until it was destroyed at Stalingrad in January 1943. Reformed in March, it was retitled *Panzergrenadier Division 'Feldherrnhalle'* in June 1943, and fought in the East from January 1944 until destroyed on the Central Front in July. It was reformed in August 1944, and sent to the East in October. Reformed into *Panzer Division 'Feldherrnhalle'* in November 1944.

90th Light (Africa) Division
Formed in August 1941, it fought in North Africa until destroyed in March 1943. (In March 1942 it had been retitled 90th Infantry Division (motorised)).

164th Light (Africa) Division
Formed in August 1942 from units in 'Fortress Crete', and fought in North Africa until destroyed in May 1943.

386th Infantry Division (motorised)
Formed at the end of 1942. Reformed in March 1943 into 3rd Infantry Division (motorised).

Panzergrenadier Division 'Feldherrnhelle'
See 60th Infantry Division (motorised).

Panzergrenadier Division 'Brandenburg'
Formed in the South-East in October 1943 from *Division Brandenburg* (which had developed from the *Abwehr* offensive Intelligence formations under Adm. Canaris) and units of Fortress Division Rhodes, and fought in the East from December 1944.

Panzergrenadier Division 'Kurmark'
Formed in February 1945 and fought in the East.

Panzergrenadier Division 'Grossdeutschland'
Formed in May 1942 out of motorised Infantry Regiment *Grossdeutschland*. Fought in central USSR until June, when it was moved to the south before returning to the centre in September. In November it again went to the south where it remained until the end of July 1943, when returned to the centre. In May 1944, it was transferred to Bessarabia and in July returned to the centre for a short time before being moved to Lithuania and Latvia in August. In December the division reformed in East Prussia, where it fought until overrun at the end of March 1945.

Although classified as a Panzer Grenadier Division, *Grossdeutschland* was in reality a panzer division with a stronger complement of tanks than any Army or Waffen-SS armoured formation. On 13th December 1944, the division was grouped with *Panzergrenadier Division 'Brandenburg'* to form the *Panzer Korps Grossdeutschland*. The division was undoubtedly the Army's most favoured formation and was arguably the finest fighting unit produced by Germany during the last war.

4th SS Polizei Division
Formed in October 1938 as an ordinary, non-motorised infantry division, it fought in the East from August 1941, and was reorganised into a panzer grenadier division in February 1943. In December it was moved to the South East, but returned to the East in September 1944.

11th Waffen-SS Freiwilligen Panzergrenadier Division 'Nordland'
Formed out of Germanic European volunteers in July 1943, it was moved to the South East in September and to the East in November. Almost completely annihilated in April 1945.

16th Waffen-SS Panzergrenadier Division 'Reichsführer SS'
Formed in July 1943 in Corsica and later in Italy. From April 1944 it fought in the South East, from June 1944 in the South West, and from March 1945 in the East.

17th Waffen-SS Panzergrenadier Division 'Götz von Berlichingen'
Formed in November 1943, it fought in the West from June 1944 until capitulation.

18th Waffen-SS Freiwilligen Panzergrenadier Division 'Horst Wessel'
Formed in February 1944 from 1st *SS Freiwilligen Brigade* (motorised) composed of Germanic European volunteers. From August 1944 it fought in the East until destroyed in December. Reformed in January 1945, it was in action in the East from March until capitulation.

23rd Waffen-SS Freiwilligen Panzergrenadier Division 'Nederland'
Formed in June 1943 from *SS Freiwilligen Legion 'Nederland'*, and was in action from November in the South-East, being moved to the Eastern Front in January 1944.

Light Divisions

1st Light Division
Formed in 1938, fought in Poland and reformed in the winter of 1939/40 into 6th Panzer Division.

2nd Light Division
Formed in 1938, fought in Poland and reformed in the winter of 1939/40 into 7th Panzer Division.

3rd Light Division
Formed in 1938, fought in Poland and reformed in the winter of 1939/40 into 8th Panzer Division.

4th Panzer Division
Formed in 1938, fought in Poland and reformed in the winter of 1939/40 into 9th Panzer Divison.

Panzer Divisions

1st Panzer Division
Formed in October 1935 at Weimar, it fought in Poland, France and the USSR, north and centre. At the beginning of 1943 it was moved to France for a rest and refit, and then to the Balkans in June. In November it was returned to the USSR, this time to the northern· Ukraine, where it was operational until September 1944, when it moved to the Carpathians. Fought in Hungary and Austria until capitulation.

2nd Panzer Division
Formed at Würzburg in October 1935, the division fought in Poland, France, the Balkans and central USSR. It remained in the Soviet Union throughout 1942 and 1943, in January 1944 withdrawing to France for a refit. It fought in Normandy, during the withdrawl across France, in the Ardennes Offensive and in the battle for the Rhine. Its remnants surrendered at Plauen at the end of the war.

3rd Panzer Division
Constituted in October 1935 in Berlin, the division fought in Poland, France and in central USSR. The division remained on the Eastern Front, fighting mainly in the south, from 1942 until January 1945 when it was moved from Poland to Hungary. It surrendered in Styria/Austria in May 1945.

4th Panzer Division
Formed at Würzburg in 1938, the division fought in Poland, France and in central USSR, where it remained until it finally retreated into Latvia in the autumn of 1944. Operational in Courland until early 1945, when sent to Germany where its survivors later surrendered to the Americans.

5th Panzer Division
This division was formed at Oppeln in November 1938 and fought in Poland, France the Balkans and in central USSR. It remained in the Soviet Union, mostly in the south, until late 1944, when it moved back into Latvia (Courland). The remnants of this division surrendered to the Soviets in the spring of 1945, north of Danzig.

6th Panzer Division
Formed in October 1939 at Wuppertal out of 1st Light Division which had fought in Poland. Took part in the attack on France and in the invasion of the Soviet Union, first in the north and then in the centre. In May 1942 the decimated division was transferred to France for a rest and refit prior to returning to the USSR in December, this time to the south. Later moved to Hungary, withdrawing to Austria in March 1945; its remnants surrendered at Brno, Czechoslovakia.

7th Panzer Division
Formed in October 1939 out of 2nd Light Division which had seen action in Poland, the division fought in France and in central USSR. In June 1942 it was moved to France where it took part in the occupation of Vichy in November. The following month the division was returned to the East, to the south this time. In August 1944 it was sent to the Baltic States where it was operational until November. Gradually withdrawing to the West, its remnants surrendered at Schwerin in May 1945.

8th Panzer Division
Constituted in October 1939 from 3rd Light Division which had been in the invasion of Poland, the division fought in France, the Balkans, and in northern and central USSR. From April 1943 it was in the south of the Soviet Union, and in September 1944 it retreated to the

Carpathian mountains, into Hungary and then to Moravia, remnants surrendering at Brno in May 1945.

9th Panzer Division
Formed in January 1940 out of 4th Light Division which had fought in Poland, the division saw action in Holland and France, the Balkans and southern USSR. In March 1944 it was moved to France to rest and refit, combining with 155th Reserve Panzer Division. The 9th fought in Normandy and in the Ardennes, its remnants being captured in the Ruhr pocket in April 1945.

10th Panzer Division
Formed in April 1939 in Prague, only a part of this division took part in the invasion of Poland—Panzer Regiment 7 and the staff of Panzer Brigade, which, with other units, formed *'Panzer-Verband Kempf'* (Armoured Formation Kempf) a temporary formation with the strength of a 1941-type panzer division. The 10th Panzer Division fought in France and central USSR. In April 1942 it was moved to France for a rest and refit, and took part in countering the Canadian raid on Dieppe in August 1942. The following December it was sent to Tunisia where it was destroyed in May 1943. The division was never reformed.

11th Panzer Division
This was constituted in August 1940 out of units from 5th Panzer Division, and fought in southern USSR until June 1944, when it was sent to the south of France for a refit and rest. There it was in action against the American and French forces, retreating to Alsace, and from there moving to the Saar in the north and to Bavaria in the south, where its remnants finally surrendered.

12th Panzer Division
Formed in Germany in October 1940, the division fought in the East in the centre from June-September 1941, north from September 1941—November 1942, centre from November 1942—February 1944 and the north again from February 1944 until the end. Its remnants surrendered to the Soviets in Courland (Latvia) in May 1945.

13th Panzer Division
Formed from a nucleus of units from 2nd Panzer Division in October 1940 in Rumania, it fought in southern USSR from June 1941 to September 1944, when it was sent in the following month to Hungary. Although destroyed in January 1945 during the defence of Budapest, it was immediately reconstituted as *Panzer Division 'Feldherrnhalle 2'*.

14th Panzer Division
Formed from elements of 4th Panzer Division in August 1940, the 14th fought in the Balkans and in southern USSR. Totally destroyed at Stalingrad, the division was reformed by October 1943 in France, and was returned to the south of the Soviet Union in November. Again suffering heavily, it was refitted in June 1944 and then sent to Courland (Latvia) in August, where its remnants surrendered to the Soviets in May 1945.

15th Panzer Division
Constituted partly from units of 10th Panzer Division in August 1940, the division, known as the 15th Light, was sent to Libya in April 1941. Later titled the 15th Panzer Division, the remnants of this formation were captured in Tunisia in May 1943. It was reformed in July only as a Panzer Grenadier Division.

16th Panzer Division
Constituted in August 1940 partly from units of 1st Panzer Division, it formed part of the reserve in the Balkan campaign. The division fought in South USSR until destroyed at Stalingrad, but was reformed in France in March 1943. After serving in Italy, it was returned to southern Soviet Union in November 1943, and withdrew into Poland and then into Czechoslovakia, where its remnants surrendered at Brno in May 1945.

17th Panzer Division
The division was formed in October 1940 and fought in central USSR until November 1942, when it was transferred to the south. It remained in the East until it was effectively destroyed in April 1945.

18th Panzer Division
Constituted in October 1940, the division saw action in the USSR, in the centre to June 1942 and then in the south, returning later to the centre. As a result of its heavy losses during October and November 1943, it was reorganised as 18th Artillery Division.

19th Panzer Division
Formed in October 1940, it fought in central USSR until April 1943 when it was moved to the south. Withdrawing across the northern Ukraine in March 1944, it was deployed in East Prussia in July, and then, at the end of the year, in Poland. In February 1945 it went to Bohemia where its remnants ended the war.

20th Panzer Division
The division was formed in October 1940 and fought in central USSR until it was transferred to Rumania in August 1944. In November it was sent to East Prussia, and then to Hungary in December, where it was captured in May.

21st Panzer Division
Constituted in February in 1941 (as 5th Light Division, to be formed into a full panzer formation in July 1941), the division fought in Libya from February until surrender in Tunisia in May 1943. It was reconstituted in France in July 1943 and was in the West until January 1945 when it was transferred to the Eastern front.

22nd Panzer Division
Formed in September 1941, it was sent to South USSR in March 1942, but was almost totally destroyed by the end of the year. Part of the division was to help form the 27th Panzer Division in September 1942, and the 22nd was ultimately disbanded.

23rd Panzer Division
Although begun to be constituted in October 1940 in France, the division was not fully formed until September 1941. In March 1942 it was transferred to central USSR and withdrawn to Poland after heavy losses incurred at the end of 1943. There it fought until September 1944 and was then moved to Hungary in October.

24th Panzer Division
Formed in February 1942, largely from units of 1st Cavalry Division, it was destroyed at Stalingrad. The division was reformed in France in early 1943 and was sent to Italy in August prior to its return to South USSR in October. A year later it was operational in Hungary, and then moved into Slovakia, where it remained from December 1944 to January 1945. The division was then transferred to West Prussia and retreated into Schleswig-Holstein, where its remnants surrendered in May.

25th Panzer Division
Constituted in February in 1942 in Norway, the division moved to France in August 1943, and to South USSR in October. Largely because it was not yet fit for action, the division suffered heavily, and was sent to Denmark in April 1944 for a rest and refit. Returning to the East in September 1944, it fought in the central sector of the front till the end of the war.

26th Panzer Division
Formed in France 1942, the division went to Italy in July 1943 where it fought until the end of the war. Its remnants surrendered near Bologna in May 1945. Because of the rugged terrain found in Italy, the division was provided with extra panzer grenadiers.

27th Panzer Division
The division began to form in France in September 1942, but was sent to the USSR before this process was complete. It was destroyed in January 1943.

28th Panzer Division
This division was formed out of 17th Reserve Panzer Division and 16th Panzer Grenadier Division in April 1944 in France. It fought in the West from D-Day until its remnants were captured in the Ruhr pocket in April 1945.

Panzer Lehr Division
Constituted in November 1943 from the demonstration units of panzer training schools, and fought in the West from June 1944 until its remnants were captured in the Ruhr pocket in April 1945.

Panzer Division 'Feldherrnhalle 2'
Formed in early 1945 from the remnants of 13th Panzer Division and *Panzer-Grenadier Division 60 'Feldherrnhalle.'* It fought in Hungary and in Austria until the end of the war.

232nd Panzer Division
An incomplete division formed in the East in February 1945 out of Field Training Panzer Division Tatra, and destroyed in March.

233rd Panzer Division
An incomplete division formed out of 233rd Reserve Panzer Division in Denmark, where it remained until the capitulation.

Panzer Division 'Norwegen'
An incomplete division instituted in September 1943 and destroyed in June 1944.

Panzer Division 'Kurmark'
An incomplete division in regimental strength formed in January 1945 out of Battle Group Langkeit. Fought on the Eastern Front till the end of the war.

Panzer Division 'Holstein'
An incomplete division, of regimental strength, instituted in February 1945 in Denmark and moved at the end of the month to the Eastern Front, where it was destroyed late in March.

Panzer Division 'Jüterbog'
An incomplete division in regimental strength. Formed in February 1945 and fought in the East.

Panzer Division 'Münchenburg'
An incomplete division in regimental strength. Formed in February 1945 and fought in the East.

SS Panzer Division 'Leibstandarte SS Adolf Hitler' (LAH)
This division was developed from Hitler's bodyguard unit which began the war as a motorised infantry regiment, becoming a division in 1941. In September 1942 it was formed into SS Panzer Grenadier Division *'Leibstandarte Adolf Hitler'*, although it possessed a tank complement which placed it above the average Army panzer division. On 22 October 1942 the division was retitled as a full panzer division.

From July 1942 to January 1943 the division was in France, and was then transferred to South USSR, where it was operational until April 1944, with only a brief period, from August 1943 to March 1944, in northern Italy and France. From June 1944 to February 1945 it fought in the West, and was then sent to Hungary. It ended the war in Austria.

2nd Waffen-SS Panzer Division 'Das Reich'
'Das Reich' began the war as a motorised infantry division (with the title SS *Verfügungstruppe Division* instituted in October 1939) and became a Panzer Grenadier division on 9 November 1942. Its tank strength made it for all other purposes a very strong panzer division, and this was recognised when, on 22 October 1943, *'Das Reich'* was redesignated as one.

From July 1942 until January 1943 the division was in France and was then transferred South USSR where it remained until March 1944. It fought in the West from June 1944 to February 1945, when, together with the LAH, it was sent to Hungary. It ended the war in Austria.

3rd Waffen-SS Panzer Division 'Totenkopf'
'Totenkopf' began the war as a motorised division (instituted after the Polish campaign) and on 9 November 1942 it became a panzer grenadier formation, although its tank strength was such as to make it a particularly strong panzer division. On 22 October 1943 it was retitled as a panzer division.

The division was in France from October 1942 to February 1943, and was then transferred to the southern sector of the Eastern Front, where it remained until the end of the war.

5th Waffen-SS Panzer Division 'Wiking'
'Wiking' was formed out of SS motorised infantry regiment 'Germania' in 1940. On 9 November 1942 it was designated a panzer grenadier division, although possessing the strength of a panzer division. On 22 October it was redesignated as a panzer division.

'Wiking' incoporated German and some Scandinavian volunteer troops, and fought in the southern part of the Eastern Front until the end of the war, except for the latter half of 1944 when it was transferred to the centre.

9th Waffen-SS Panzer Division 'Hohenstaufen'
Instituted on 31 December 1942 as a panzer grenadier division, 'Hohenstaufen' was designated a panzer formation on 26 October 1943. First operational in Poland in April 1944, it was transferred to the West in June, where it remained until moved to Hungary in March 1945. The rest of the division surrendered in Austria in May.

10th Waffen-SS Panzer Division 'Frundsberg'
Formed on 31 December 1942 as a panzer grenadier division, it became a panzer division on 4 November 1943. 'Frundsberg' fought in Poland from March to June 1944, when it was transferred to the West. There it remained until February 1945, when transferred Pommerania, its remnants surrendering to the Soviets in Saxony at the end of the war.

12th Waffen-SS Panzer Division 'Hitlerjugend'
Formed in 1943 as a panzer grenadier unit, it became a panzer division on 30 October of same year. 'Hitlerjugend' saw service in the West from June 1944 to the end of January 1945, when it was moved to Hungary. Its remnants surrendered in Austria at the end of the war.

Panzer Division 'Hermann Göring'
Formed in mid-1943 out of the panzer grenadier division of the same name, which had been instituted in 1942. It served in Sicily and Italy until transferred to the East in July 1944. In August it fought in Poland, but in October was withdrawn to East Prussia, where it remained until the end. In October it was grouped with a panzer grenadier division to form the Paratroop-Panzer Corps 'Hermann Göring'.

Although one of the Luftwaffe's ground formations, the 'Hermann Göring' nevertheless came under the control of the Inspector-General of Armoured Troops from March 1943.

Panzer Groups and Panzer Armies

Panzer Group 1—formed out of XXII Army Corps on 16 November 1940 and lasted until 5 October 1941. Fought in the USSR, south, under *Generaloberst* von Kleist.

Panzer Group 2—formed out of XIX Army Corps on 16 November 1940 and lasted until 5 October 1941. Fought in the USSR, centre, under *Generaloberst* Guderian.

Panzer Group 3—formed out of XV Army Corps on 16 November 1940 and lasted until 31 December 1941. Fought in the USSR, centre, under *Generalobersts* Hoth and Reinhardt.

Panzer Group 4—formed out of XVI Army corps on 15 February 1941 and lasted until 31 December 1941. Fought in the USSR, north and centre, under *Generaloberst* Hoepner.

Panzer Group Kleist—temporarily formed for the attack on the West; in existence from 10 May-30 June 1940; reformed for the attack on the Balkans, 6 April-beginning June 1941.

Panzer Group Hoth—temporarily formed during the attack on the West, 13 May-30 June 1940.

Panzer Group Guderian—temporarily formed during the attack on the West, 5-30 June 1940.

Panzer Group Nehring—temporarily formed out of 5th Panzer Army in Tunisia, from 17 November-3 December 1942.

Panzer Group Eberbach—temporarily formed out of Panzer Group West from 10-21 August 1944.

Panzer Group Africa—formed out of the German Africa Corps under Rommel from August 1941-30 January 1942.

Panzer Group West—formed in the West under *General der Panzertruppen* Geyr von Schweppenburg and, later, *General der Panzertruppen* Eberbach, from February-10 August 1944.

1st Panzer Army—formed out of Panzer Group 1 on 5 October 1941 and served in the East until the end of the war.
    Oct 1941—Jul 1942 under control of Army Group South
    Jul 1942—Feb 1943 under control of Army Group 'A'
      (south USSR)
    Feb—Mar 1943 under control of Army Group Don
    Mar 1943—Apr 1944 under control of Army Group South
    Apr—Oct 1944 under control of Army Group North
      Ukraine
    Oct 1944—Feb 1945 under control of Army Group 'A'
    Feb—May 1945 under control of Army Group Centre

Commanders:

Generaloberst von Kleist	5 Oct 1941–21 1942
Generaloberst von Mackensen	21 Nov 1942–5 Nov 1943

Generaloberst Hube	5 Nov 1943–21 Apr 1944
Generaloberst Raus	21 Apr 1944–15 Aug 1944
Generaloberst Heinrici	15 Aug 1944–20 Mar 1945
General der Panzertruppen Nehring	20 Mar–8 May 1945

2nd Panzer Army—formed out of Panzer Group 2 on 5 October 1941 and served in the East and in South East Europe.

Oct 1941—Sept 1943 under control of Army Group Centre
Sept 1943—Dec 1944 under control of Army Group 'F'
   (South East Europe)
Dec 1944—May 1945 under control of Army Group South

Commanders:
Generaloberst Guderian	5 Oct 1941–22 Dec 1941
Generaloberst Schmidt	22 Dec 1941–15 Jul 1943
Generaloberst Model	15 Jul 1943–15 Aug 1943
Generaloberst Rendulic	15 Aug 1943–25 Jun 1944
Generaloberst Böhme	25 Jun 1944–Oct 1944
General der Artillerie de Angelis	Oct 1944–8 May 1945

Note: While in South-East Europe, 2nd Panzer Army had no panzer or panzer grenadier divisions under its command.

3rd Panzer Army—formed out of Panzer Group 3 on 31 December 1941 and served in the East until the end of the war.
   Dec 1941—Sept 1944 under control of Army Group Centre
   Sept—Oct 1944 under control of Army Group North
   Oct 1944—Jan 1945 under control of Army Group Centre
   Jan—Feb 1945 under control of Army Group North
   Feb—May 1945 under control of Army Group Vistula

Commanders:
Generaloberst Reinhardt	31 Dec 1941–16 Aug 1944
Generaloberst Raus	16 Aug 1944–10 Mar 1945
Generaloberst von Manteuffel	10 Mar–3 May 1945

4th Panzer Army—formed out of Panzer Group 4 on 31 December 1941 and served in the East until the end of the war.
   Dec 1941—May 1942 under control of Army Group Centre
   May—June 1942 under control of Army High Command
      (as reserve)
   June—Jul 1942 under control of Army Group South
   Jul 1942—Feb 1943 under control of Army Group A
   Feb—Mar 1943 under control of Army Group Don
   Mar 1943—Apr 1944 under control of Army Group South
   Apr—Oct 1944 under control of Army Group North
      Ukraine
   Oct 1944—Feb 1945 under control of Army Group A
   Feb—May 1945 under control of Army Group Centre

Commanders:

Generaloberst Hoepner	1 Dec 1941–8 Jan 1942
Generaloberst Ruoff	8 Jan–31 May 1942
Generaloberst Hoth	1 May–15 Nov 1943
Generaloberst Raus	15 Nov 1943–21 Apr 1944
General der Panzertruppen Nehring	21 Apr–1 May 1944
Generaloberst Harpe	1 May–28 Jun 1944
General der Panzertruppen Balck	28 Jun–20 Sept 1944
Panzer der Panzertruppen Gräser	20 Sept 1944–8 May 1945

5th Panzer Army—formed on 8 December 1942 out of XC Army Corps, and served in Tunisia until destroyed on 13 May 1943. Reconstituted on 21 August 1944 out of Panzer Group Eberbach and served in the West until the capitulation.

Dec 1942—end Feb 1943 under control of High Command South
end Feb—May 1943 under control of Army Group Africa
Aug—Oct 1944 under control of Army Group B
Oct—Nov 1944 under control of Army Group G
Nov 1944—Apr 1945 under control of Army Group B

Commanders:

Generaloberst von Arnim	8 Dec 1942–9 Mar 1943
General der Panzertruppen von Vaerst	9 Mar–13 May 1943
General der Panzertruppen Eberbach	21–23 Aug 1944
Oberstgruppenführer und Generaloberst der Waffen-SS Dietrich	23 Aug–12 Sept 1944
General der Panzertruppen von Manteuffel	12 Sept 1944–6 Mar 1945
Generaloberst Harpe	9 Mar–17 Apr 1945

6th SS Panzer Army—formed on 6 September 1944 and served in both the West and in the East

Sept 1944—Feb 1945 under the control of Army Group B
Feb—May 1945 under the control of Army Group South

Commanders:

Oberstgruppenführer und Generaloberst der Waffen-SS Dietrich	6 September 1944–May 1945

11th Panzer Army—formed on 28 January 1945 and served in the East under Steiner. In March it was renamed Army Group Steiner.

Panzer Army Africa—Formed out of Panzer Group Africa on 30 January 1942 and continued until 23 February 1943, when it was renamed the 1st *Italian Army*

Commanders:

Generaloberst Rommel	30 Jan–9 Mar 1942 (followed by sick leave)

General der Panzertruppen	
Crüwell	9–19 Mar 1942
Generalfeldmarschall Rommel	19 Mar–22 Sept 1942
	(followed by sick leave)
General der Panzertruppen	
Stumme	22 Sept–24 Oct 1942
General der Panzertruppen	
von Thoma	24–25 Oct 1942
Generalfeldmarschall Rommel	25 Oct 1942–23 Feb 1943

NOTE   *Generalfeldmarschall*—Field Marshal
Generaloberst—Colonel-General
General der Panzertruppen—General of Panzer Troops
General der Artillerie—General of Artillery

Epilogue

The men of 29th Panzer Grenadier Division held Coriano ridge during fighting which took place in Italy during the Autumn of 1944, and defended this key position against assaults launched by a succession of British and Commonwealth forces.

As a Company runner carrying a message to battalion headquarters I crossed this stricken ground during the Gothic Line battles and was shocked at the evidence of how bitter had been the fighting. One memory is always with me. Two soldiers, one from the Welch Regiment of my own Division, the other a Panzer grenadier of 29th Division, stood locked in death, connected by the rifle and bayonet with which one was transfixed. Dead grenadiers surrounded one slit trench from which it was clear that a Bren gunner had held out, while British dead, from several regiments, were lying in front of another small trench which a heap of used cartridge cases indicated had once held a machine gun post. The desolate scene evoked memories of pictures I had seen of fighting of the First World War and the frightful loss of life which had been sacrificed for a geographically unimportant but militarily vital piece of ground.

And there in Italy, in September 1944, savage and desperate battles were raging and the northward thrust of my own Division was being obstructed by the tenacious defenders of an ordinary panzer grenadier division. If these would fight so desperately for a low ridge in Italy how fanatically, I asked myself, would the first-class panzer grenadiers of the elite units fight on high mountain peaks as we of 8th Army advanced upon our final objective, Vienna?

Contemplating, while sheltering from the fury of a short barrage, the sad sights of the Coriano battlefield, I thought that these panzer grenadiers could and might make the war last for ever. They certainly did their best and I would honour the panzer grenadiers of 29th Division by using as their epitaph the motto of my own Regiment; 'Pristinae virtutis memor'—'Remember the courage of him that is fallen'.

J. S. Lucas

Bibliography

Akademiya Nauk   Istoriya SSSR   Moscow 1973

Barclay C.   The history of the Duke of Wellington's Regiment. 1919–1952   Clowes. 1953

Bird W.   No retreating footsteps. The history of the North Nova Scotia Regiment.   Kentville Pub. Co. Nova Scotia. 1956

Bullen R.   The history of 2/7 battalion The Queen's Royal Regiment   Besley & Copp Exeter. 1948

Fort Garry Horse   Vanguard: The Fort Garry Horse in the Second World War   C. Misset NV Holland. 1945

Hastings J.   The Rifle Brigade. 1939–1945   Gale & Polden. 1950

Haupt W.   *Heeresgruppe Mitte*   Podzun Verlag 1967

HQ 2nd Army   An account of operations: Vol. 1   HQ 2nd Army. 1945

Hughes F. K.   A short history of the West Riding and Midland Infantry Division (TA)   Stellar Press. 1957

Institut Marksisma   Istoria Velikoi Otechestvennoi Voinni Sovietskovo Soyuza. 1941–45 Tom 2 and 5   Moscow 1963

Jackson G   Operations of 8th Corps   St Clements Press 1948

Krafft J   *SS Panzer Grenadier Ausbildungs- und Ersatz Bataillon 16, in den Kämpfen bei Arnheim*   Unpublished photostat

Lemelsen J   *29 Division*   Podzun. 1965

Meyer K   *Grenadiere*   Schild Verlag. 1957

Müller-Hillebrant B.   *Das Heer 1933–45* (3 Vols.)   Mittler und Sohn. 1968–74

Official history of the Canadian Army in the Second World War. Vol. II. The victory campaign   The Queens Printer Ottawa. 1960

Ressik D   The Durham Light Infantry at War   DLI Depot

Ryan C   A bridge too far   Simon & Schuster

Senger und Etterlin Dr F. von   *Die Panzergrenadiere*   Lehmanns Verlag. 1961

Taurus Pursuant: A history of 11th Armoured Division   1945

Schramm   *Die Geschichte des Panzer Korps Gross Deutschland. Band III   Traditionsgemeinschaft.* 1958

Phillipi-Heim   *Der Feldzug gegen Sowjet Russland*   Kohlhammer Verlag Stuttgart. 1962

Seaton A   The battle for Moscow   Rupert, Hart, Davis 1971

USMA   A military history of World War II   US Military Academy. Washington 1953

Wagener C.   Moskau. 1941   Podzun Verlag. 1966

War Diary   25th SS Panzer Grenadier Regiment. June–July, 1944   Unpublished photostat.

Weidinger O.   *'Das Reich' Division. Band III*   Munin Verlag. 1973

Woude U. J. D.   *Arnhem. Betsiste Stad*   J. Veen's Verlag Amsterdam. 1945.

Together with letters, war diaries and interviews.

Index

EQUIPMENT

General